T6117849

24 Things
You Can Do with
Social Media to Help
Get into College

To my mother.

Every daughter needs a hero,

Every woman needs a confidante,

Every mother needs an ally,

Every writer needs a reader.

Thank you for being mine!

24 Things
You Can Do with
Social Media to Help
Get into College

Gina Carroll

TURNER
PUBLISHING COMPANY

Turner Publishing Company
Nashville, TN
www.turnerpublishing.com

24 Things You Can Do with Social Media to Help Get into College

Copyright © 2010

All rights reserved.
This book or any part thereof may not be reproduced or transmitted in any form or by any means,
electronic or mechanical, including photocopying, recording, or by any information storage and retrieval
system, without permission in writing from the publisher.

Library of Congress Cataloging-in-Publication Data

Carroll, Gina L.
 24 things you can do with social media to help get into college / Gina L. Carroll.
  p. cm.
ISBN 978-1-59652-748-5
1. Universities and colleges--Admission--United States. 2. College applications--United States. 3.
Social media--United States. 4. Online social networks--United States. I. Title. II. Title: Twenty-four
things you can do with social media to help get into college.
 LB2351.2.C37 2010
 378.1'610285--dc22

2010030476

A reputation for a thousand years may depend

upon the conduct of a single moment.

~Ernest Bramah

The way to gain a good reputation

is to endeavor to be what you desire to appear.

~Socrates

Contents

Introduction

Introduction

You've worked very hard to submit your best college application. You've invested the years of committed high school study and months of filling out your forms. You've chosen the right faculty members to submit strong recommendations and you've written and edited your essays to perfection. You've clicked "send" to forward that carefully crafted application on to your college of choice. And now the admissions officer has your application in his hands. But that's not all he has. As he reads your application, he has your Facebook page up on his computer screen. It's easy for him to quickly look from paper to Facebook profile to determine if what you are representing online is consistent with the positive picture you've painted in print. One admissions officer I interviewed (who asked to remain anonymous) said that he often finds that the Facebook information detracts from the image an applicant puts forward on paper. He admitted that he has (on more than one occasion) decided against the applicant based on negative online information.

Other stories have been surfacing to indicate that this admissions officer is not alone. We've heard rumors about the high school students who, because of some inappropriate pictures or content on their Facebook pages, had their college admissions revoked, and about the admissions officers who used information on Facebook to decide between two graduate school candidates. Regardless of the frequency of these stories, college admissions officials acknowledge that they are in fact utilizing the whole array of Internet social media in order to connect with, get informed about, and choose prospective members for their entering classes.

You do not want all of your college application efforts to be compromised by your information on social networking sites and other social media.

For most people, the term "social media" means Facebook and MySpace, those extremely popular social networking sites that are cyber-home to a huge and ever-growing number of people—young and old. But social media includes a whole universe of other sites and activities online—blogs and micro-blogging sites (like Twitter), community networks and forums—where people are meeting, aggregating, and carrying on conversations short and long. If you are applying to college, chances are you are of the age to be considered a "digital native." That is, you were born into the computer age and you know your way around the Internet. Chances are you are already well familiar with social media and are an active participant. You are apt to be one of the estimated 400 million people with a Facebook account,[1] among the 18 million folks who use Twitter, and among the 12 million who write blogs or the 57 million who read them.[2]

Until very recently, these social media have been primarily a way to connect with friends and family and be a part of online exchanges across the Web. Now, you, as a native, are fortunate to be among the first students to have a whole new way to find and connect with colleges and universities worldwide right from your desk or laptop. Universities and colleges—big and small, public and private—are not just using the Internet to dig up dirt on their applicants. They have discovered the value of social media for attracting and communicating with prospective students. They recognize that in order to learn more about the digital natives who are their applicants, they must meet them where they are—and they (you) are overwhelmingly on the Web.

In addition, the Internet has spawned an entire cottage industry of social media–based Web sites designed to facilitate your college search and admittance. From SAT and ACT exam assistance to organizing your school search to showing you the ins and outs of college life, these online services provide an exhaustive array of tools to help you along your college quest.

Given that the Internet offers so many tools for you to discover colleges and for them to find you, it makes sense for you to use your social networks and sites as platforms to put your best face forward in the application process. Through an integrated effort with your Facebook profile, personal blog, and special interest networks, you can build a more detailed, personal, and multi-media presentation that gives schools a more complete picture of what you have to offer. With forethought and planning, you can use your social media skills and tools to reach the admissions offices of your colleges of choice like never before, presenting them with an enhanced, positive view of who you are and what you can contribute to their campus communities.

A Simple Plan

A Simple Plan

Because most universities and colleges are now investing considerable time and energy in social media, so should you. The more positive and proactive you are online, the better your chances will be for attracting the schools of your choice.

You need a plan. And with all that you already have to do for your college admissions, your social media plan should be simple. This book offers 24 things to help you formulate and institute a simple plan. By following the 24 suggestions, your plan will address three goals:

- Goal #1: Find your soul mate school. You will use online resources to define your college search based on your interests and preferences so that you can determine a short list of great college matches for yourself.

- Goal #2: Showcase your gifts and talents. You will create an online presence that only shows your best side—the real you—your highest self. You will learn the dos and don'ts of social network reputation building.
- Goal #3: Make connections with your college choices. You will chart out your method for getting on the radar of your target schools. You will optimize online conversations and exchanges in order to connect with college admissions offices and express your interest.

The following 24 suggestions assume that you have already established a social network account and have a presence on Facebook (or a similar network). If you have not yet ventured into the social networking world, do not worry. You do not need to stop reading and join. There will be time along the way to set up your account. If you do have an account already, you will be spending your time redesigning and improving your information so that your profiles are attractive and meaningful to admissions officers who may come by to visit. The same is true for your other online homes—your Web site, blog, and college network profiles.

Once you complete these 24 things, the social media part of your college application package will be one of its strongest components. And you can rest assured that you have taken the steps necessary to build a positive picture of yourself for colleges to discover online.

Note to Parents

"Social media has changed the landscape of college admissions." So says the first statistically significant study on how college admission offices are using social media recently published by the University of Massachusetts Dartmouth Center for Marketing Research.[1] And its findings indicate that colleges and universities have outpaced Fortune 500 companies with their use of social media to reach their target audience—your college-bound teenager. Unlike Fortune 500 companies, who seek, for the most part, to reach adults, admissions offices want to connect with the best and the brightest among this generation of digital natives.

If you are currently raising a high school student, you are in a special place in history. By now you already know that your children get and use information in ways vastly different from those you used as a high schooler. The interconnectivity and hyper-communication that characterize your kid's reality are what has likely created a chasm of misunderstanding between you and your child . . . and what has inspired you to exclaim—

"Doesn't anyone research in the library anymore?" or

"Why haven't I met your 'friends'?" or

"This is not how I applied to college!"

We are, at the moment of this writing, right at an exciting and slightly nerve-wracking juncture, where colleges have decided to jump onto the social media bandwagon by shifting their focus and resources to their online presence. The UMass/Dartmouth study indicates that 85 percent of colleges use at least one form of social media to reach students, but their policies are still in the formative stages. And as is the nature of the Internet, social media will likely continue to rapidly evolve and change, so it is difficult to know exactly what to do. There are three things parents can know for sure:

1. Since colleges have acknowledged that they review their applicants' social media in the decision-making process, applicants who have a social media presence should invest some time making their presence work to their advantage and not to their detriment.

2. On the other hand, college admissions officers state that they do not have the manpower to search out and review every applicant's online accounts. So if your child is not currently

on any social media network, blog, or forum, neither your child nor you should feel pressure to sign on just to be found by a college. An applicant does not get extra points for being on Facebook. In fact, right now most admissions personnel claim they only go online primarily for two reasons: (1) they encounter a strong indication that a candidate's social network content will greatly illuminate the candidate, or (2) that the online information will show something so negative as to necessitate the candidate's exclusion from consideration.

3. The college admissions industry online is a vast and ever-growing universe of information. Many of these college-related sites have also embraced the social media model to attract your student. You and your child can pick and choose the places you want to either park or surf in order to get the insight you need for college decisions.

So parents, take a deep breath (help your child take a deep breath) and follow the Simple Plan in a way that works best for your family.

Best of luck!

The 24 Things

The College Search—
Finding Your Soul-Mate
School

The College Search—Finding Your Soul-Mate School

Only a handful of universities and colleges seem to get all of the attention. In terms of media coverage and word of mouth, most of us tend to hear only about the Ivy League schools, the sports powerhouses, or our local, hometown colleges. Even when we expand our vision, we often rely on the schools that appear on the much-publicized ranking lists, like the *U.S. News & World Report*'s list of the top 400 U.S. universities[1] and colleges or *Princeton Review*'s list of the top 371 colleges in the country.[2] These lists vary and offer insights based on a variety of factors and criteria—the *U.S. News & World Report* list focuses on a school's comparative prestige, while the *Princeton Review* list zeros in on the student experience. When you encounter these lists, you may be overwhelmed by the choices or discouraged by the high standards of admissions. Four hundred schools may seem like a lot to consider. But there are far more university and college choices than these. And since the factors that are most important and pertinent to one person may be very different than for another, your list of top colleges may look very different from these published ones. In light of this reality, there are two things you should remember:

1. There are likely far more choices than you know. There are more than 7,000 institutions of higher learning in the United States. And these schools represent a wide range of standards and requirements, as well as a huge variety of environments and academic offerings. In other words, there is a cornucopia of choice. Not only is there a college or university ideally suited for you, there are several.
2. So don't panic. There is no need to get over-whelmed by the numbers and choices. You can

begin to sort through and eliminate choices based on your particular interests and preferences until you have a short list of schools to consider.

The great news is there are lots of wonderful new Web sites to help you explore and sort, once you have determined the school characteristics that you prefer. So let's get started.

— 1 —
Find the Right Size Campus

Do you want to be part of a large campus where many of your classes contain several hundred students and you can study in relative anonymity? Or would you prefer to be part of a small, close-knit community where your entering class is just a few hundred students and academic classes are more intimate?

School and class size can make a huge difference in your day-to-day college experience. Your life on a campus with 50,000 other students will vary considerably from one where there are only 3,000. You may already know that you do better academically when your professors know you personally and you have open access to them. This is easier to achieve on a small campus. Or you may want to mix it up with a large variety of students. You might be a huge sports fan and seek the big stadium, big game experience, and the greater choice of activities that come with a sizable population and a larger campus.

If you need help thinking about the right match for you, don't forget to talk to the people who know you best, both academically and socially. Your parents, school counselor, or advisor and even your friends may provide some insights about your personality and life-style preferences.

Searching for schools based on specific criteria has now been greatly simplified by college review sites. A college review site is a Web site networking service that offers a whole menu of information and information-gathering tools. The social network component of these sites is generally two-tiered. The first tier is made up of a group of current college students who can join the site as contributors and post a variety of content about their colleges. The second tier is made up of prospective students who can become registered users. In this way, the prospective student can create a profile and use the profile page to collect information and links about various colleges. They can also interact with current students through forums and question-and-answer pages. The strength of these sites is their extensive databases of college stats, facts, and comparisons and the ability to store your college search results in one place. The fun part of the experience is when the two tiers interact and share and exchange information in real time.

College Prowler (www.collegeprowler.com) is a great example of a college review site. (See a list of other college review sites in Appendix 3: 24 Places to Go Online in the back of this book.) Once you register on the College Prowler site, you can fill in information about yourself and your college preferences. Then you can search for schools based on your criteria. On College Prowler's college search page (http://collegeprowler.com/finder/), you can enter the school size you desire to search. You are not required to register to use this function, but if you are registered, you can save the results and get an automatic feed of information about the schools of your choice on your profile page. The search function allows you to search for schools from 0 to 40,000 and up. To find small campuses, you might search 0 to 2,000 as your range. For a medium-sized school, search 2,000 to 15,000. And for larger schools, you might search 15,000 and up. You can choose any range. The results show up immediately on a grid, which allows you to link to the school's profile page. Once you've reviewed the school, you can add the school to your "My Schools" list on your profile page, for later comparison with your other choices.

As your list grows, you can continue to fine-tune it with other criteria. College Prowler and some other sites allow you to connect your account with Facebook. The interface with Facebook allows for an exchange of information between sites to save you time and effort. It is particularly useful in three ways. You can log in to the review site using your Facebook log-in information. Some sites will auto-fill your review site profile with the information you have already entered on Facebook to save you time and repetition.

And the connection between the sites allows you to share the results of your review site searches and lists on your Facebook page. Thus, if you choose to use more than one review site, you can combine the information from the multiple sites onto your Facebook page for more convenient comparisons and analysis.

The size of your college is an important factor. But it is only one of many you must consider as you are trying to compose your short list of choices. *Wall Street Journal*'s Abby McCartney warns that the question of size can be misleading. She suggests in her article, "When Choosing A College, What Really Matters?" featured on the Unigo.com college review site, that the more important question is how the school deals with its size. McCartney says:

> If it's big, do students break down into smaller communities based on dorms, majors or activities? Do deans and professors go out of their way to get to know students? If it's small, does it share resources with neighbor-

ing schools? How hard is it to find a class
or activity that the school doesn't offer?[1]

The point here is not to throw away your search
results based on size alone, but to keep in mind that
once you have created a list based on all of the criteria
important to you, you don't necessarily have to nix
a school that meets most of your requirements just
because its size is wrong. That school may do a good
job of accommodating for its size disadvantages.

– 2 –
Find the Right Location

Do you want to attend school in your hometown or have set your vision on a campus far, far away? You may envision bringing your laundry home for the weekend. Or you may feel that even your parents coming to visit you on "Parent Weekend" would cramp your style! In addition, you may be seeking to escape the cold winters of home for a warmer location, or you may want to experience the changing of the seasons and living in a winter wonderland. For some students, their primary interests require that they be in a certain location. If you want to study marine biology, for example, you may want to be near an ocean. If your interest is in business, you may choose an urban center, where job and intern choices are greater. Some students prefer the hustle and bustle of a city, with greater cultural offerings and activity, while others prefer a more rural environment that has a slower pace and fewer distractions.

You should not underestimate the importance of a school's location and setting to your overall happiness once you get there. This consideration goes beyond the campus environment to the surrounding community. Narrowing down your school choices by location and setting is a snap with social media tools.

First, go to the college review site that you have picked and use the search function to generate a list of schools based on location and setting before you do a size search. This will depend on how important the location and setting criteria are for you. If location and setting trumps size, you should generate a new list with the location or setting criteria along with your size requirement. Then add to your list accordingly. If size is more important, then refine your already existing list with location and setting searches.

At StuVu.com, you can search by state or by miles from your zip code. In addition, you can search by campus setting—rural, suburban, town, or city. This site also allows you to connect by way of Facebook. StuVu offers student created photos, videos, and reviews. So once you've got your list of schools, you can visit the campus profiles on this site and view pictures of campuses and the surrounding areas. Each StuVu profile has an "Around Campus" section that provides information and student ratings for "local flavor," as well as restaurants, hotels, nightlife, shopping, local services, and coffee and tea spots.

Second, with your refined list of schools, you can expand your research by gathering facts about the weather and the surrounding setting from the school's own Web site and the myriad travel sites online.

A college's official Web site is a great source of information. Most schools have invested considerable effort making their Web sites accessible, helpful, and full of facts about the school. This is often a good jumping off point when you are ready to look at the campus and its setting. The University of Houston Web site, for example, under their "About" tab, includes this nice summary about the city of Houston and the university's interaction with the city:

Houston is the nation's fourth largest city and an international destination, bursting with energy. Known as the energy capital of the world, the city is home to 19 Fortune 500 companies and the world's largest medical center—providing limitless opportunities for UH students to develop their skills in internships and fieldwork experiences in the real world.

Houston's quality of life and proximity to research partners in business and government also make the city an attractive home for talented professors and their families.

Houston is a fun place to live, too. Interested in the arts? Take in a performance of the Houston Ballet, Houston Grand Opera, or Houston Symphony, or wander through Houston's Museum District. Rather be outdoors? Choose from more than 160 golf courses, commune with wild animals at the Houston Zoo, or go hiking at the Armand Bayou Nature Center.

"A mouth-watering destination for foodies," according to *USA Today,* Houston offers dining options from BBQ to seafood, and from Tex-Mex to Vietnamese. Jazz and blues clubs add to the lively nightlife. As Dan Halpern wrote in the *New York Times,* "Maybe that's what makes Houston such an unusual and wonderful place—there are so many different Houstons to see."[1]

These sections give a good introduction to the city that surrounds the school and what to expect there. But remember, a college's Web site is its primary marketing tool. The school endeavors to present its strengths and primary attractions and those of its surrounding city or town. Often, its weaknesses are minimized or missing. You'll notice that the University of Houston's discussion about its city is missing any mention of the local weather. And since Houston gets severely hot and humid for a large part of the school year, Houston's weather is a factor most prospective students would want to know about. So although the college Web site might be a good place to start your investigation, you should not stop there.

To get a thorough discussion about a geographical location, social networking sites devoted to travel are very informative. What's great about the travel social networking sites is that most of the reviews and posts are written by locals, who endeavor to give the inside scoop about their town. VirtualTourist.com, for example, provides the following lists (with links) : Things to Do, Local Customs, Nightlife, Shopping, Transportation, Sports, Tourist Traps, Warnings and Dangers, and General Tips. In addition, the site offers location-specific forums and several contributors who post about living in the particular locale. Many contributors include their own pictures. These sites are full of insights and ways to connect with the locals who may not be connected to the college or universities in their towns. In all, they offer you more of the good and bad news about the city or town you are investigating, which gives you a broader perspective. The Virtual-Tourist.com contributors who wrote about Houston weather discussed Houston's extreme heat, hurricane history, and propensity to flood. One contributor said:

> You don't often think of Southern U.S. cities for extreme weather, but Houston's weather can be nasty—especially in the summer. Thunderstorms and rain can be very heavy, but it's the summer heat & humidity that'll really get you. The locals call them 90/90 days—90 degree heat, 90% humidity. Houston is the only place where I've been in a swimming pool—and sweated. I thought I saw the pool water on the boil![2]

You are not likely to find this kind of frank discussion on the college's own Web site.

YOUniversityTV.com is another helpful Web site for investigating school locations. YOUniversityTV.com is a college information site that has a handy map function that shows a large map of the United

States, with markers for cities and colleges. You can click on a city and see what schools are in the area. You can click on the school markers and be directed to the school profile. This map is particularly helpful for seeing what colleges are in a given area.

Safety Note: Since the travel sites are not university related and are not designed with under-aged users in mind, they tend to be monitored less stringently. Students should proceed with caution. Be conservative about signing up and be restrictive about the personal information you provide, especially in forums. For a more complete discussion about online safety, go to Appendix 1: A Word About Safety.

— 3 —
Find the Right Specialty

If you already know or have a strong inkling about the course of study you are interested in pursuing in college, it makes a lot of sense to refine your list of schools by matching your interests with the schools' academic specialties. However, before you invest hours researching academic specialties and majors, consider these three things:

1. Universities are called universities for a good reason. They are immense centers of learning where diverse academic pursuits take place. Almost every school has much more to offer than you will uncover, even when you are on campus. And most have majors and disciplines you have never heard of. Now is not the time to try to wrap your arms around the vast array of

your choices. Just let your interests guide you and know that part of the college experience is discovering the many paths of study and inquiry your interests can take you.

2. Don't worry yourself right now if you do not yet know what you want to study. Most liberal arts schools give you one or two years to declare a major because they know that even if you think you've decided what you want to do, you don't yet know enough about the school's offerings and options to make an informed decision. Even students who have a burning passion for a subject find that, when faced with the wonderfully diverse and dizzying array of choices, they often change to a course of study that better addresses their interests. This is how the process should work. You should let your interests and passions guide you, but you should also be open to what you find once you get on campus and gain more exposure.

3. Some students come to college with the goal

of quickly settling on a major, completing the requirements, and getting out. They have a four-year plan to finish up, get the degree, and graduate as quickly and efficiently as possible. Other students view college as an opportunity to find themselves and discover their passions. They have a slower, less hurried approach. They plan to try a few majors, take full advantage of the extracurriculars, and saturate themselves with the total college experience. If this takes a little longer than four years or five years or six, so be it. Both of these methods have their merits, but they also both leave some benefits on the table. If you are in too much of a hurry, you miss some beneficial and fortifying experiences that round out your education and increase your marketability as a job prospect in the future. But if you meander too long, you take the risk of losing your way, failing to find a focus, and expending unnecessary resources before you are through. Striking a balance between these two approaches is what you should be striving for. As you are searching for your college destination, keep this balance in mind.

For students who have a clear notion of what they want to study, there are great online ways to investigate what schools are doing in specific areas. One exciting social media tool for this purpose is YouTube EDU. This education section of YouTube amasses the videos of an impressively long list of participating universities. The videos include a wide range of activities and subject matter—including lectures, faculty presentations and Q & A's, interviews with students, and admissions and campus information. YouTube invites two-year and four-year colleges and universities that have established a YouTube channel to participate. The material presented on the school's channel must be educational and not promotional, so the focus of these videos is what is happening on campus academically. The site is set up to allow searches by school name, but what is ideal for our purposes is that the sidebar category index divides the videos by subject matter. This makes a search for schools by interest simple. The following subject matter is clickable:

- Business
- Education
- Engineering
- Fine Arts & Design
- Health & Medicine
- History
- Humanities
- Journalism & Media
- Law
- Literature
- Mathematics
- Science
- Social Science

Within each section is a diverse offering of material. In the Business section, for example, UC Berkeley has a series of statistics lectures and a discussion by campus guest, Bill Gates, talking about philanthropy and "giving back." In the Humanities section, University College London has posted a video about conserving fragile coastlines, and the University of Oklahoma features "OU in Arezzo" showcasing their international programs. Once you have zeroed in on certain schools, you can go directly to their YouTube channels and get a picture (literally) of their goings-on across campus departments and interest groups.

Often students catch wind of certain professors who have gained some notoriety and acclaim for the work they are doing in their area of expertise. YouTube EDU is a good place to locate any video of those professors. If you have an interest in psychology and you've heard of the hugely popular and highly esteemed Stanford University professor Phillip Lombardi, you can search his name in the YouTube EDU general search bar and several (upwards of 19) results show up. There are videos of his lectures and class presentations; videos of him discussing his most famous experiments (and video of the experiments themselves); videos of students talking about their experiences in his class; and videos of interviews with him. The video presentation of faculty, their accomplishments, and teaching styles (where you can actually see them in action and in context) enhances your search in ways a written description cannot.

In your college search-by-interest process, it may be helpful to look at how faculty is regarded in the departments of your interest. For general information about the quality of professors at a given school or in an academic department that interests you, you can plug into RateMyProfessors.com. This site boasts coverage of more than six thousand schools, one million professors, and ten million opinions. This is a networking site, which allows current students to register and set up an account so that they can add critiques of their instructors based on "overall quality," "easiness," and if they are "hot." Needless to say, these ratings should be taken with a grain of salt, but extraordinary professors tend to stand out on this site. If they are exceptionally good or difficult or uncaring, students are motivated to take the time to critique them. And thus, those professors tend to have a large number of ratings. You can go to a school's profile page on this site and get a general idea of how students on campus feel about the faculty at large, by department, or individually.

− 4 −
Find the Right Student Body

Some experts argue that this is the most important criterion. College is not just a continuation of your current high school experience. Your college years represent your transition from a child to an adult. As I have mentioned, your college years will be a collection of experiences that will define who you are and what direction your life will take. So what happens outside the classroom will be just as important.

In college, you no longer have the highly structured learning environment you have become accustomed to in high school. In high school, the average student has 35 to 40 hours of actual class time per week. In college, class time can be reduced to 15 to 20 hours per week. College leaves you with a lot of unstructured time outside the classroom, and you will be on your own to figure out what to do with it. This is the big college life question—how will I spend my free time? And a huge part of this question is—with whom?

You may start your investigation of campus life and students by looking at the numbers. You have already sorted your schools by population size. But what are the characteristics of that population of students?

When it comes to campus life explorations, Unigo.com, as a review site, is a one-stop shop! The site boasts one of the largest number of college student reviewers among the college review sites. Founder Jordan Goldman says that on many campuses his company has amassed reviews from 5 to 10 percent of that school's student population. Unigo's impressive college student participation is part of Goldman's mission of providing college applicants with more honest and updated information about college life. The college profile pages on Unigo.com offer a summary of the school that covers all of the most sought-after criteria. The summary is based on current student comments and reviews. The true power of Unigo, however, is the Student Review Finder function. Because the site has collected so many reviews, you can search for reviews from certain students that fit your interests and share your characteristics. For example, if you want to read college reviews from students of a certain major, you can narrow your search accordingly. You can also search by gender, race, extracurricular activities (like sororities or sports), political leanings, and home state. This makes your investigation of school life extremely efficient. Another helpful feature of the student reviews is that each review provides some biographical information on the reviewer, including what other schools he or she applied to. This is helpful for finding student opinions from students with a similar background to yours.

The student reviews on this site can be brutally honest. You do not just hear from students who are happy with their college choices. For example, on the Unigo.com site, Elon University has 46 reviews. Although most of the reviews were positive, citing the campus's beauty, small class sizes, and caring faculty as highlights of the university, this sophomore reviewer expressed overwhelming disappointment:

> I go to a school 1,022 miles away from my home and family. I have to spend 12 hours traveling in order to spend 24 hours at home. My professors don't believe in giving A's, so the extraordinary amount of money I pay for my education reflects an average GPA for all the hard work I do. My sorority doesn't have a real house because the school can't provide all its organizations with equal housing. Greek Life doesn't believe in social functions. And I'm convinced Elon isn't a real college. Don't go here if you want a real college experience.[1]

CollegeProwler.com offers some unique college functions, as well. Their "Do You Stand a Chance?" application calculates your chances of admittance to the schools on your list based on your GPA and standardized test scores. This function is, of course, just an estimate based only on partial information. It essentially compares your scores and a short list of your extracurricular activities with those of the current school population. This allows you to see where you would fit academically among the students of a particular school. The application does not consider the other parts of your application (like essays and recommendations), so the results really should not be given much weight other than as a ballpark comparison.

CollegeProwler.com also provides a "Personality Quiz" that is designed to help you match your "true self" with the right school environment. This is a fun exercise to get you thinking about what is important to you socially and environmentally, so that you can seek out a compatible school. I took the test and received the following results:

Social Butterfly

You scored "Social Butterfly" because you are outgoing and fun.

Your ideal school is a big school in a big city that has hot guys, good nightlife, and great shopping.

Uniform: Your uniform is a skirt, a strappy tank top, and sandals.

Playlist: You rock out to "Low" by Flo-rida and T-pain and whatever's playing in the club.

Books: You like to read anything gossip-related.

Movies: Your favorite movies are *The Notebook* and *How to Lose a Guy in 10 Days*.

Room: Your room is filled with clothes, shoes, and pictures of you and your girls.

Hobbies: You like shopping and going out with your girls.

Food: Your favorite food is a big salad.

Necessities: You won't leave home without a compact, lip gloss, and your cell phone.[2]

If this kind of information would be helpful to your search, the quiz takes two minutes. There is no deep analysis happening here. On your profile page, the "Do You Stand a Chance?" and the "personality test" applications merge with the school list that you've generated from your searches and tell you by percentage your chances of admittance and how well your personality matches up with each school. Use these applications as fun ways to generate suggestions for schools that you may not have noticed or considered.

Another place to zero in on campus life is the perennial social media favorite, Facebook. Facebook was founded originally by Harvard college students whose initial mission was to bring college students together both among students on their individual campuses and between the different colleges across the nation. Given that history, college students have been using this revolutionary social media tool to form groups with common interests. The formation of groups continues to be a very active use for

Facebook. A Facebook Group represents a Facebook page that members join if they want to connect with others over a common interest, particular theme, or cause.

Facebook has a number of groups that might interest prospective college students. Students new to the college application process might find the college acceptance groups interesting. Although you will want to join a college acceptance group only after you have received your acceptance letter, you can still read the pages of these groups to see the kinds of students a certain school is accepting. These groups are very popular and active, so lots of conversation takes place. The new admittees talk about their admissions processes; discuss what they like and dislike about the school that has admitted them; and ask questions about student life on campus. These can be interesting and informative exchanges for students beginning the application process. The acceptance groups for some schools date back several years. To find Facebook groups, go to your Account Tab and click on Application Settings and then Groups. You can search the groups directory using the search window on the top left of the page.

– 5 –

Plan a College Tour—On Campus or Online

Campus visits have traditionally been a very important part of the college search process for applicants. Students find the firsthand experience of walking the campus and interacting with school personnel, faculty, and students very helpful and influential to their ultimate school choice. In a 2008 survey conducted by the College Board, 72 percent of the students surveyed said they became much more interested in the colleges under their consideration through college visits.[1]

Campus visits are also an important way to officially express your interest to an admissions office. Because colleges and universities receive so many applications, they try to determine (and focus their efforts) on the applicants who are truly interested in their school. Most admissions offices weigh a campus visit heavily in this assessment. Typically, you are asked to schedule a visit so that the admissions office can connect with you and document your visit while you are there. Once on campus, you are usually asked to fill out a candidate form, meet with admissions officers, and take their official tour.

If you decide to take a college trip, you can plan and schedule your campus visit online before you go. Most schools provide visitor information on their official Web sites. The admissions pages of these sites provide details for scheduling an appointment with admissions personnel, tours of campus, and any special accommodations for prospective students. Some schools offer on-campus programs specifically designed for applicants, like Stanford University's Discover Stanford. Discover Stanford is a two-visit opportunity for students interested in applying to the school. The first visit is designed for high school juniors and seniors. The first portion is a one-hour session led by the Admissions office, in which students learn about the admissions and financial aids processes. The second part is a walking tour of campus. You are asked to make a reservation online at http://www.stanford.edu/dept/visitorinfo/tours/prospective.html. Other schools, like Wesleyan College, offer visitation events throughout the year. Wesleyan has three such events: a Fall Preview Weekend in October that is open to high school seniors. It is a free, overnight opportunity to learn about the school. Junior Day takes place in March and is offered to high school juniors and their families as an introduction to campus life and the admission process. Pioneer Weekend is available to admitted students to afford them a taste of life at the college. In addition, the school has an Open Saturday program, where high school students can visit campus, meet with an admissions counselor, and take a tour. This event happens about seven times each year. In order to participate in any of Wesleyan's visitation opportunities, students can fill out a Campus Visit Request Form online at http://www.wesleyancollege.edu/Admission/Undergraduate/Visit/

ScheduleaVisit/tabid/319/Default.aspx.

Although summer may be the most convenient time to visit schools, it's best to visit when they are in session. You may find during your family vacations or other travels that you want to stop by a nearby campus. If you have not made an online reservation, you should still connect with the admissions office and document your visit with them, so that they know that you made the effort. This is very important!

If you find that you cannot visit schools in person, or you can only visit one school when you have more than one you'd like to see, you can accomplish the next best thing with a virtual college trip online. As you plan your online "visit," make sure you keep in mind the same two goals you'd accomplish with an actual trip to the campus—to see how the campus feels to you and to connect with the admissions office to get your questions answered and to express your interest.

There are a number of ways to get a comprehensive visual tour of colleges. Most college official Web sites offer beautifully produced videos and slideshows of their campus highlights. You will want to see those presentations. But you will also want to get real-time visuals of how campus is being experienced by current students. The following steps are a suggested way to use the social networks online to get a total campus tour experience:

1. Visit the school's official Web site and take all of the virtual tours that they offer. Many schools offer lots of pictures, slideshows, video, and guided presentations. They often use virtual tour Web sites to house their visual tours. So the official Web site employs many different options for you to see and experience the campus.
2. Go directly to a college tour site, like Campus-Tours.com or YOUniversityTV.com. Campus-Tours.com offers software to help colleges and universities create online tours. The site houses the tours and also provides a college profile of

extensive facts about the university or college. From CampusTours.com's school profiles you can click on a tour, the school Web site, a map, and photos. YOUniversityTV.com allows you to register, create a profile, and collect school tours on your profile page. The YOUniversityTV.com tours include much more than just the location and setting. The videos discuss the admissions process and numbers, the surrounding area, financial aid, housing, fields of study, and campus life. On their videos, you hear from admissions officers and administration, faculty, and students. The videos also highlight the school's history, areas of renown, and well-known faculty and alums. As you watch the tours, write down your questions.

3. Go to YouTubeEdu.com and go to the You-Tube channel of your school of interest. Then search the channel for videos of class lectures and faculty presentations. If you know of a particular professor in your area of interest,

search by name or department. View a variety of classes and presentations. Often you can observe a small class lecture and a large auditorium lecture. Emory University's YouTube channel, for example, has a small group class where a music professor discusses the difference between a sonata and a cantata. They also feature a series of lessons to a large audience by the Dalai Lama. Emory's channel has a wide variety of presentations from students speaking about their majors and even Arnold Schwarzenegger's graduation commencement speech. Let your interests be your guide as you surf the video selections of the school channels that you choose. Many schools provide videos about their food service, dining halls, dorm life, and social scenes.

4. Connect with your schools of interest when their admissions representatives visit your town. College admissions officers are assigned territories so that they can be sure to reach and

recruit students from all over the nation. When those officers come to visit a town or region, they usually participate in local college fairs and high school visits. Your school college counselors have a schedule of college visits to your campus and to citywide fairs. Check with your counselor to see when your schools of interest are going to be in town. Plan to be present when they come. If you meet an officer at school or a fair, make sure that you fill out a student interest card or form for them.

5. If your college of interest grants interviews, request an interview in your hometown as part of your application process. When you meet with a school representative (in an interview or at a fair), tell them that you are unable to make a visit to campus, but you have already done all of the virtual tours online. Then inform them that you have specific questions based on all of the information you've gathered online and elsewhere. Show that you have done your

research and be able to articulate why you are interested in their school.

6. Participate in a Virtual College Fair. Chapter 6 discusses how to do so.

– 6 –

Attend an Online College Fair

The online college fair is another way to connect with your schools of interest when you cannot meet them face-to-face. Like the college campus visit, traditional college fairs are important ways to gather information and to connect with admissions officers to express your interest. Individually, most admissions personnel are not very accessible through social media because in being so they would become inundated with requests and inquiries. So the online college fair is a rare opportunity to connect with an actual person in the admissions office.

CollegeWeekLive.com is a virtual college fair platform that hosts events centered on live chats with college admissions officers. The site has three big fairs each year. Their large events boast representatives from 250 schools and 50 states. They also offer regional fairs year-round. In May, for example, a Texas fair is scheduled, where all participating colleges and universities in Texas are showcased. The college fair screen looks like a large exhibition hall with each school represented with its own "booth." Each booth houses a video presentation of the school, like the virtual tours discussed in Chapter 5. At each booth, you can enter a chat room and ask questions in real time with a representative from the school, usually admissions personnel. When you register and attend a fair, you can get a certificate as evidence of your participation.

This site has other events for prospective students. Colleges sponsor student chats, which are exchanges between a current student and an admissions officer. Registrants can submit questions during these sessions. Some schools also offer seminars that showcase some of their academic departments or majors, while others provide informational videos about admissions and financial aid. The strength of this site is the focus on interaction and exchange. The real-time question-and-answer sessions are a powerful way to connect with real people on campus right now. Like the other college information gathering and review sites, you can save these videos, presentations, and documents to your profile page for future reference and comparison.

When you plan to take part in the live chat sessions, as with any interaction with admissions officers, you should spend some time preparing beforehand. As you have taken your tours, watched videos, and perused the review sites, you should be writing questions as they come up. Now is not the time to be a silent observer. Make sure you ask a question or two. Remember one of your goals is to get on the radar of the admissions offices of your school of choice. So it's important to be an active participant.

Another online fair site is VirtualCollegeFairs.com. VirtualCollegeFairs.com has a different approach. Their concept is more like an ongoing college fair, as opposed to CollegeWeekLive's scheduled real-time events. When you register and log in to VirtualCollegeFairs.com, you get access to college "booths," which are similar to college profile pages. What distinguishes this site is that some of the booths provide contact information (name, email address, and phone number) for the school's admissions office. In addition, they have a "talk back" feature that allows you to send questions to the admissions officer listed and have your questions answered through the site. Not all of the schools with booths provide contact information, however. The smaller, lesser-known schools offer access to their admissions offices, while the larger schools provide basic contact information that can be found on their own official site. Few of the large schools offer the "Talk Back" feature. For the fully participating schools, you can also request that your profile information, which is basic school and test score stats, be sent to the school. So even though this site is not as interactive as CollegeWeekLive, it does offer another way to connect with schools and contact admissions personnel with questions and expressions of interest.

The online college fair is an efficient tool for directly communicating with your schools of interest. The CollegeWeekLive.com events offer the closest simulation of an actual face-to-face encounter. But because they are scheduled events, they require planning and forethought on your part. Make sure you register for the site and keep current on its calendar of events.

If you choose to take part in a virtual college fair, currently the best course of action is the following:

1. Join CollegeWeekLive and mark your calendar for the upcoming events.

2. Make sure you register for the fairs you want to attend.

3. When you attend, be prepared to ask questions and get your certificate of participation.

By now, you should have a clearer idea of what

your soul-mate school looks like, and you have probably found some interesting prospects. You've reviewed a lot of schools and sorted through your choices to make and refine your short list. And you should have taken the steps to tour your schools of interest either online or on campus, and to make contact wherever possible, both official (filling out interest forms) and unofficial (fairs and high school campus meetings).

Using Social Network Sites to Show Your Best Side

Using Social Network Sites to Show Your Best Side

Social media is designed to help you find, attract, and draw people to you. It is meant to optimize your online connections. Each component is intended to reflect who you are and what you like, so that you can connect with other like-minded people. Most Facebook members, for example, are not just connecting with anyone. They are deciding who they want to interact with and who they do not. In other words, social networking sites are tools for reaching target groups of people. Companies and scores of enterprising individuals have harnessed Facebook's effectiveness at finding target audiences for their products and services. Businesses have incorporated Facebook into the marketing of their brands for this reason. The American Marketing Association defines a "brand" as:

A name, term, design, symbol, or any other feature that identifies one seller's goods or services as distinct from those of other sellers. The legal term for brand is trademark.[1]

In a sense, even those of us who are only interested in finding friends and family are branding ourselves, too. We are crafting our Facebook pages to show certain aspects of ourselves to attract and engage certain people. Your brand is your image and your reputation—what you stand for and what makes you distinct. For purposes of college admissions, you need to be very deliberate and intentional about what is included on your page and what is not.

– 7 –

Learn the Rules of Engagement

In order to control what appears on your Facebook page, you should be very clear about all of the ways information ends up there. By now, if you are a longtime Facebook member, you know what constitutes each information section of your profile. But let's look at them with an eye toward building your brand and see how they can be used to affect how you appear to a college admissions official who may come to visit your page.

The idea here is to look at each component of a Facebook page and think about who is in control of that content, where that content goes on Facebook and beyond, and how that content is seen by others.

Home Page: Your homepage is seen only by you. It contains your News Feed, which shows all of your

Facebook activity and the activity of your friends. This includes all of your status information and that of your friends. The right sidebar helps you manage your page and communications. From here, for example, you can link to your Messages, Events, Photos, and Friends. You can also grab applications and games that you can add to your page. Finally, the bottom of the sidebar displays who among your friends is currently online. This page is your private space and is useful to keep tabs on what new information has been added to your Facebook pages that might not be private, like pictures and comments to your status updates. What you decide to share with visitors on this page shows up on your "Wall."

Your Wall: Depending on your privacy settings, there are four places visitors can go on your wall. Your wall shows all of your Facebook activity and the activity of your friends (your News Feed). It is a snapshot of your Facebook world. If someone has commented on your page, it shows up here. All of the places you go on Facebook and every word you have written also show up here. If a person wants to get an idea of how active you are on the network, this is where they would come. Since all of the content that you have added as "Status" information shows up on your wall and your friends can add comments to all of your status updates, you are not in complete control of the content that may appear here. You may only control who can see this information through the privacy settings. You can decide that you want to restrict all of your status comments with a global privacy setting or you can decide before you add a status comment whether you want a different privacy setting for that particular comment. Chapter 19 offers a full discussion of how to maximize your privacy settings.

Your Profile Page: This page allows you to input your personal information—your likes and your favorite things. The "Basic Information" section permits you to post your current city of residence, your hometown, birthday, and your chief relationships (whether you have children, your marital status).

At the bottom, you are asked to answer a question: "What are you looking for on Facebook?" Your choices are "friendship," "dating," "a relationship," or "networking." This information appears to your friends on the "Info Page."

Herein lies the Facebook conundrum for the college applicant. The whole purpose of Facebook is to connect with people in order to build relationships of your own choosing. This is why your Facebook page is such a good place to discover who you really are, or perhaps more important, how you see yourself. It may seem unfair for colleges (and others) to use this essentially private medium to judge you. But really, when it comes down to it, colleges that utilize Facebook as a socially based evaluative tool really do fit Facebook's relationship-building purpose. Colleges want to know if you are a good match for their school and their population of students. In short, although "To Get Into College" is not one of the what-are-you-looking-for choices, you, as a college applicant, now have to proceed as if it is. Afterall, you want to connect with your soul-mate school just as much as the school wants to connect with you. You can decide to keep all of your information private, but this requires careful management of your privacy settings and your friend requests. Even if you choose to restrict access to your personal information, there are no guarantees that your information will not be viewed and shared beyond your desired audience. None of the college admissions officers I interviewed have any problem gaining access to the Facebook pages they seek to view.

Your safest bet as a prospective applicant is to carefully and thoughtfully fill out all of the information choices.

Under the "Likes and Interests" section, be sure to fill in all of the categories. These prompts are very similar to the personal information sections of some college applications. So don't be afraid to express your true likes, dislikes, and passions, especially if they are unique and diverse. Fill these categories up with your information, so that a college visitor to your site can see that you have well-developed interests and pursuits.

Under the "Education and Work" sections, make sure to add any jobs that you currently hold. Colleges like to see enterprising and engaged prospects.

The "Contact Information" tab gives you the opportunity to enter all of the ways you can be reached. I strongly recommend that you not include an address or a phone number (unless your parents approve). For safety purposes, you do not want to make yourself so easily found. See Appendix 1: A Word About Safety for a thorough discussion of safety and privacy considerations.

The "Contact Information" section does, however, give you the opportunity to list your URL information. So if you have a Web site or a blog, you can include the link here. This is a great way to direct your college visitor to the other places you are showcased online.

The Right Sidebar: The Right Sidebar includes a summary of your information—a quick view of personal facts about you. It features your profile picture, your statement, and basic "About Me" information. Your friends are also listed here. If you have linked to any other Web site, these are listed on your side-bar, as well. This link information acts, for college admissions purposes, as another little summary of the online places and subjects that interest you. The links are collected from your status posts.

Your Photo Page: This page houses all of your photo albums. If you are like most teens, this is the highlight of your Facebook experience. The photo pages of young Facebook users tend to be very dy-namic—ever growing and changing. Photos show up here in two ways. The first, of course, is when you upload your own pictures. The other is through your friends. If your friend has a picture with you in it, he or she can "tag" you, and the picture will appear on your wall and on your photo page.

Your Video Page: The same is true for video. If you have uploaded video, this is where visitors can find it. You can also be tagged on the videos of friends.

Your Link Page: This page lists all of your status comments that include a link to another URL location. If you like to comment about music or sports sites, art or hobby articles or Web sites, you can amass a nice list of link history here. Any visitor who is interested in what you like and where you go online will be particularly interested in this page.

Third Party Pages: If you have connected your Facebook page to any other site or service, a tab for that site will appear along this tab bar. So, for example, if you signed onto the CampusBuddy.com college review site and connected your CampusBuddy profile to Facebook, you can designate a separate Tab on your Facebook page for CampusBuddy. The information you've input at CampusBuddy becomes a part of your Facebook information, including your high school courses, test result information, what colleges you are interested in, and so forth.

Your Searchable Public Profile: Your public profile is what anyone can see who searches for you on Facebook or a search engine. This profile is an abbreviated version of what you have listed on your Facebook profile page. The public profile shows your name, profile picture, and lists of things you like based on the pages or groups you have joined on Facebook. It provides up to four columns of your "Likes," such as movies, television, stores, and non-profit organizations. And depending on your privacy settings, the public profile may show the profile pictures of some of your friends.

The Facebook page is an incredible resource for anyone interested in knowing more about you. If you want to make this information available to colleges, you will need to manage it by carefully choosing what information appears on the different pages and tabs, and by reviewing the information often, to remove any unwanted content that has been added by your friends. You should be deliberate about the privacy settings you choose—which information will be seen by the public and which by your friends only. You can attempt to restrict a school's access to your information by using the highest privacy settings, but do not assume that these restrictions are foolproof. If you have lots of friends and third-party applications feeding in and out of your account, the information is more easily accessible. Your safest course of action is either to remove your Facebook account altogether or make it a tool for showing your gifts, talents, and the wonderful person that you are. With a little planning and attention, as discussed in the next chapters, you can craft your Facebook page to present a positive brand that is appealing to the schools that you want to attract.

And although Facebook is currently the most popular social media destination, there are other very active sites to utilize. If you are currently using MySpace, you can apply these suggestions to your MySpace page. Lots of people are committed to MySpace for the tools it offers that Facebook does not. For example, musicians and music lovers feel that MySpace is superior for "instant streaming" music. And many MySpace devotees believe that the friending system is more fluid on MySpace, allowing easier movement within the network. However, the consensus seems to be that MySpace has a lower standard of privacy and security controls than Facebook, so parents tend to feel that Facebook is a safer environment for their teens and perhaps themselves. If you are a MySpace member, all of the suggestions contained herein apply to the MySpace medium as well. MySpace has even more content options and applications that are unique to it. It offers, for example, a blog page option, where you can create a full content blog. Just keep in mind, on any social network, management of page content streams becomes more challenging and impactful as the number of streams increases.

Chapters 12 through 18 will discuss other social media tools you can use to impress college admissions folk and attract them to you, such as your own Web site or blog, common-interest network sites (like Ning), and forums. Each of these offers opportunities to put your work, accomplishments, and passions out into the Internet sphere. But each has important safety and privacy concerns that you should make sure you know. Before you invest your private information, know what audience is involved and exactly how your information can be used and disseminated. Every site sets forth its own policies with regard to use, security, and privacy. Do your homework.

— 8 —

Pick the Perfect Profile Picture

How important is a picture in the application process? How important is the visual representation of a fat, juicy hamburger to a fast food commercial? How important are dreamy panoramic vistas in the travel guide of your next vacation? How vital are the profile photos of the person who has just invited you to friend them on Facebook? You get the idea. Very important!

We all know personally how powerfully images can influence our thinking and decision making. We are emotionally affected by visual representation. What we see greatly influences how we behave—both positively and negatively. Study after study shows that we humans have a propensity to judge others based on appearance. We use how a person looks to decide if that person is a guilty criminal, a good doctor, a worthy politician, an appropriate mate, or a trustworthy business partner.[1]

We know that college admissions offices utilize photos to help them form better, more complete portrayals of their candidates. For this, most schools request a photo with each application. Fortunately, your school application offers much more information by which a school can assess you. The picture you include with your application will likely be of a formal nature denoting the seriousness of your application and your desire to relay an air of dignity and intelligence. You most likely will submit a posed photo, like your high school senior year portrait.

But the situation is much different for your social media profile pictures. These pictures tend to be very informal and candid snapshots. Since the social network profile page (or even a blog) is very personal, readers search out your photo to go with your content. Thus choosing a perfect profile picture is a very dynamic exercise. And since social media content is constantly changing, social networkers also change their profile pictures often. Bloggers tend to keep the same picture on their "About Me" sections. On Web and blog sites, profile pictures are often less prominent on the page. But since they are often the only clear representation of the owner of the site, they are just as important. Chances are, admissions personnel will be visiting your Facebook page or blog after they have read over your application. They will likely be looking for information that validates and reinforces the positive information you have stated on that application. Your profile picture will likely be the first thing they are drawn to on your page. The following suggestions will help you make sound decisions about what pictures to choose for this important visual representation on all of your social media.

1. Two Safe Choices: The safest choices for a profile picture are either a portrait or a personality shot. A portrait is a picture that only features your face or a close-in shot of you. It

might show your whole body. But generally, there is no other person or object in the picture with you. This portrait does not need to be formal. In fact, for Facebook and MySpace, a more casual or event-specific shot (like a prom picture) is more in keeping with the Facebook environment for teens and young adults.

2. The Personality Shot shows you engaged in an activity that is important to you. For example, if you are a volunteer tree planter, include a close-up picture of you holding a sapling. Or if you are a musician, choose a photo of you with (or maybe even playing) your instrument.

3. Choose a picture where you look your best. Studies show that *if you want to be judged more positively, you should use a picture that portrays you relaxed, with good posture,* looking neat, stylish, and energetic.[2]

4. Also, smile. Choose a picture in which you are smiling. Research shows that a smiling face engenders positive feelings in people who view it.

Humans have a natural preference for a smiling face. You want to show yourself looking happy. Even pictures of people in full laughter are positive. Morose, angry, and snide expressions create subconscious feelings of discomfort, dissonance, and distrust in the viewer. You want your picture to inspire positive feelings in your admissions visitors.

5. Save the pictures with friends for your gallery photos. For college admissions purposes, the best profile picture is one that focuses on your face and has very little else in the frame.

A Word About Gallery Photos

The number of photographs amassed by some Facebook users can be awe-inspiring. The galleries of many Facebook teens contain more than 3,000 photos. This is quite a lot of pictures to manage. Though an admissions official will not likely sift through this many photographs, you want every single picture to say something positive about you—and not just that you have a multitude of friends or go to a lot of parties. Make sure you create galleries of pictures that showcase how you spend your time pursuing your interests and passions. You should have a variety of pictures that show the different areas of your life—school, social settings (including friends and family), work, hobbies, sports, and community service.

For social networking sites, you can organize your photos into related-theme galleries, so that they are easily accessible. In case a visitor wants to see you in action as a volunteer or an athlete, group your pictures so that with one click into an organized gallery they get the full visual story.

For blogs and Web sites, using photos to enhance your posts is a great way to draw attention to both. The ability to incorporate a multimedia approach on your site shows your visitor that you are truly committed and engaged in the endeavor.

If a picture is worth 1,000 words, what are 3,000 pictures worth—you do the math! You really can create a thorough portrayal of who you are and what you stand for. Just make sure all of those pictures conjure up only good messages about you. Chapter 20 discusses more about how to clean up your inappropriate photos and how to keep your galleries positive.

– 9 –
Highlight Your Interests
and Passions

We already know that colleges want strong students. Grades on college preparatory courses, admissions test scores, and high school grade point average are uniformly the most critical factors colleges weigh in order to admit you. You must be a good and committed student in order to succeed in college. But colleges also want to know that you have achieved something outside the classroom. All of the application and interview questions are geared toward finding what kind of person you are intellectually and how industriously you spend your time.

Although your extracurricular activities are not so important as your academics to the admissions determination, what your life looks like outside the classroom can have a profound impact on a school's decision. So it's important to know how schools use the information about your activities and your life in the admissions mix.

Through the admissions process, colleges endeavor to achieve a number of directives. They seek to build a freshman class that will be able to handle the academic rigors of college study and at the same time contribute to their campus environment in beneficial ways. Every college and university has two basic communities—its campus community of current students and faculty and its larger, worldwide community of alumni, parents, and former and affiliated faculty. Both of these communities are greatly invested in the success and prestige of the institution. Both of these communities take the well-being and reputation of the school very seriously. And therefore, both of these communities are heavily invested in the admissions process.

Colleges want to make sure that each entering class will fit into the larger and smaller school communities by contributing committed intellectual pursuit and diversity of background and interests. Colleges and universities want new admittees to be their future laureates, Noble peace prize winners, academy-award-winning directors and actors, and statesmen. They also want them to be happy members of an engaged and cohesive student body.

In light of these considerations, an applicant may feel pressure to show that he or she is good at everything. He may feel that his personal record must reveal a stellar student who is engaged in a million different activities and getting awards in them all. She might think schools are looking for an excellent generalist. In reality, colleges are more drawn to the specialist, the student who has found one or two areas of interest that have captured the student's passion and imagination. Instead of an application that asks, "Tell us everything that you can do," colleges are more interested in the questions What do you love? In what have you become an expert? What is your talent? What is it that you want to do most with your time?

In addition, colleges are looking for uniqueness

and originality. In the enormous pool of college applicants, what is it that makes you stand out? How did you get your unique perspective? What about your upbringing and life experience makes you different? How have you come to be who you are?

In the college application process, then, your goal is to highlight not just your strengths, but your individual passions and life experiences that make you distinctive and interesting. What will you bring to the college or university mix?

As a digital native and a social network aficionado, you likely have a better picture of your likes and dislikes, strengths and weaknesses than college applicants who have come before you, because social networks are perfect vehicles for sorting out who you are. The exercise of filling out your profiles requires that you think about and list information about yourself in a way that focuses on what is important to you.

In order to give a college admissions visitor a clear and consistent view of who you are, you can take the following steps:

1. Look at the information that you have on your profiles already and decide whether or not it is a consistent representation of your interests and your areas of expertise. On your Facebook page, does your "Likes and Interests" section show all that you do in the areas of your interest? For example, you might have "tennis" listed in your "Activities" box. But you should also include your tennis teams, where you play, and your tournament wins. Or if you are a violinist, don't just list "violin" in your "Interest" box. Include the last three places where you were a featured soloist or competition winner and upload a video of your best performance onto your video page.

2. There are three catch-all places where you can include the details of your interests on your Facebook page. When editing your profile page, go to "Likes and Interests." The "Activities," "Interests," and "About Me" boxes are where you can list all of your activities and

accomplishments. Make sure you fill out all the categories under the "Like" and "Interests" tab, making sure that the prompts that address your particular interests are especially well developed and chock-full of information about what you love.

3. Make sure your picture galleries show the things you are doing. Have a different gallery for each of your favorite activities. If you are a football recruit, use your social media to house your highlight films and photos. When you contact coaches, give them your Facebook link, so that they can see your film and all of the other ways you are exceptional.

4. If you have a personal blog or Web site, put the link on your Facebook page. If your written work, artwork, video, or sports information is on another site, make sure you put the link in more than one place on your Facebook page— like under "Contact Information" and perhaps the comment box under your profile picture.

5. Join related Facebook Groups. Facebook has thousands of special interest and theme groups that you can join. They are small (some are large) communities that communicate about a certain topic. These groups can be a good way to talk about your interests and share resources and information about the things that you love. To explore different Facebook groups, go to your "Account" tab and click on "Application Settings" and then "Groups." If you do a search in Groups, you will find a wide variety of categories and subcategories. You can search music, entertainment and arts, sports and recreation, geography, business, organizations, student groups, and "Just for Fun." The student groups have lots of college-related interest groups. You can join groups that appeal to you with a mind toward joining those that contribute to the interests you are showcasing on your page.

6. Remember, your goal is to create a Facebook

page that shows consistent pursuit and mastery of your passions. Also, be sincere about what you like. If your number-one passion is the Lakers basketball team and you have been a fan for years, then show what you have done with that passion. You may have formed a national fan club online or volunteered for the Lakers' favorite foundation. Maybe you make your own franchise-approved Laker T-shirts and have created a small business out of your trunk. Colleges would want to know about your devotion, creativity, and ingenuity in connection with your passion for your team. If you have not yet parlayed your passion into action, log yourself off of Facebook and do something about that right now!

– 10 –
Make Your Status Entries and Posts Meaningful

College admissions personnel understand that your social media Status updates are generally intended to be lighthearted and casual communications. They know that the intent of Facebook is to allow members to immerse themselves in the culture of their generation and their own self-cultivated communities. According to many college admissions officials across the country, the last thing they want to inspire is artificial social media pages that are designed solely to impress them. The very reason admissions decision-makers are drawn to social media is that they believe they will discover the true, unguarded student in his or her own element. This book is not intended to encourage the creation of artificial social media for college admissions purposes. It is, again, to help you bring your best self forward online. That best self needs to be a real person.

On Facebook, the central focus of a person's page is the "Status" post, which is a response to the prompt, "What's on your mind?" On MySpace, the prompt is, "What do you want to share?" Since your page shows a full history of your Status posts, a visitor can see what's been on your mind for several days running. Though you do not need to stage artificial posts in the name of making an impression, you should think about what you want to say and whether or not it engenders positive and responsible feedback from your friends. Since you can include links, pictures, and video to your Status posts, you really can and should make an effort to share meaningful and engaging places to go elsewhere online. Even your casual statements about how you are feeling or your commentary about current events should be stated in your most articulate and expressive manner.

Showcase your humor, even if it is silly, biting, or heavily sarcastic, but eliminate anything that seems mean-spirited. With regard to your communications and comments on the Status posts of others, make sure you exhibit restraint, compassion, and empathy. There is nothing wrong with expressing criticism or disapproval, as long as it is articulated intelligently and without cruelty. The most important thing to remember is to think before you post. Follow the ten-second rule when you encounter something that you feel warrants an emotional response. Count to ten with ten long breaths and then type your response. Before you click "Share" or "Send," count to ten again. If you still think the comment is wise and rea-sonable, send it. Colleges want to see that you have interpersonal skills and relationship savvy, that you can be a cohesive contributor to a school community and not a divisive influence, so show maturity in your online communications. If you do not have something meaningful, helpful, or supportive to say, wait to post until you do.

You should also use your Status posts to an-nounce your upcoming events or activities. If you are going to run a marathon, you should post it. After you have completed the race and know your results, post those, too. Attach a video if you have it. This may seem like bragging or self-promotion, but it isn't. You are simply letting your visitors know what you are up to and the outcome. Your friends should be people who would support your interests, help you, and cheer you on with their comments. If they are not, you may want to reconsider who is among your friend group. Chapter 21 provides more discussion about friending wisely.

You can also use your Status posts to share and comment on current events. Share what you are reading and hearing about your areas of interest. Use the link function to share news and related information online—that is, your favorite Web sites, blogs, fan sites, and other related Internet destinations. If you are involved with the relief effort in a war-torn country, for example, link to the organizations you work with; other sites that discuss the conditions and needs of the country; and other people who are writing about your or similar efforts. In this way, you show that you have genuine concern and an ongoing interest in helping and recruiting others. And once you have found other people with your interests and expertise, add meaningful and supportive comments on their Status posts, pictures, and videos. Just remember to be respectful, as we have discussed. Your history of comments on the status posts of others appears on your page, as well.

– 11 –

Utilize Applications to Tell Your Story

The world of social media applications is a playground of opportunity for users who want to add more information and gadgetry to their profile pages. Applications can be used to further customize your page to show and tell more about yourself and to connect with people and sites that share your interests.

Facebook has a whole universe of applications available. The best way to find the entire application directory is to go to http://www.facebook.com/apps/directory.php. Another way to find applications that are more likely to be of interest to you is to go to your Facebook Home Page and click on the right sidebar where "Applications" is listed. This will get you a listing of the applications all of your current friends are using. This might be a good starting place to search.

A Facebook Application Case Study

   Sandra has had a Facebook page for some time, but with college applications in mind, she wants to add to her pages to further pursue and display her interests. She has already thoroughly filled out her personal information, where she discloses three of her favorite passions. She is a jewelry maker and an animal lover. She has a large family to whom she is very devoted. She has discovered that the bracelets she makes are very popular with her friends. They feature homemade beads with likenesses of celebrities decoupaged on them. She has decided to sell the bracelets and donate the profits to the World Wildlife Fund. She currently has 895 Facebook friends, mostly from her large public high school where she is a junior. We are able to learn all of this information from her Facebook profile, status posts, pictures, and comments.

   She now wants to add some applications to enhance her page. These are the steps she might take:

1. Go to the Facebook Applications Directory.
2. Focusing on one interest at a time, scan the categories. So for her jewelry-making business, she can browse the business category, where she will find the following applications:
   a. Marketplace: this app would allow her to buy, sell, and trade with her Friends, Friends-of-Friends, and the Facebook community. She could list her jewelry here and allow her community to see her products and buy or trade for them.
   b. Promotions: If she sets up a fan page for her jewelry, this app would allow her to run interactive promotions on her Fan page. She could do sweepstakes, contests, coupon giveaways, gifting, and other business marketing activities to help her spread the word about her bracelets.
3. She may also find helpful apps for displaying her jewelry. In the Utilities category, Sandra can do a search for "slideshow" and she will

find a number of apps that allow her to use photos on her profile as a tab or a box in order to display her wares (such as Slide Show by Andre Dejavu, Magic Slide Show by ReKoo, Slide Show Creator by Slide Show Creator, and Photo Browser by Luen Ti).

4. If she is really committed to promoting and selling her jewelry, she can download Payvment E-Commerce Storefront by Payvment, which is an app that will allow her to set up a full storefront on Facebook.

5. Now she wants to add some applications that will assist her with her raising awareness about the World Wildlife Fund and coordinating volunteer efforts. She might find these apps helpful:

   a. Causes by Causes Exchange: This is an app that allows an individual activist, as well as larger groups, to mobilize their network of Facebook Friends around a cause.

   b. Cause Effect by Concentric Sky: This app

allows you to promote donations through shopping at certain sites, where a portion of the proceeds go to a charity that you designate.

6. She could also add the Social RSS Feed application, by which she could feed the World Wildlife Fund's Web sites and YouTube channel directly onto her Facebook profile. In this way, she and her friends would have the benefit of WWF information without leaving Facebook. She could also decide if she wants every new WWF post to automatically appear on her Wall as a Status post.

7. As an animal lover, Sandra could tap into myriad pro-pet applications available for downloading:

    a. Dogbook, Catbook, Horsebook, and even Rodentbook by Poolhouse allow you to create online profiles for your favorite pet.

    b. Save a Dog by DogTime.com provides an app so that you can join in the effort to keep dogs out of shelters and find them good homes. The app allows you to become a "virtual" foster parent to a dog that needs adoption and enables you to encourage your Facebook Friends to do the same.

8. Sandra has lots of applications to choose from under the family category.

   a. FamilyLink by FamilyLink.com: Currently, this is the most popular family app. With FamilyLink, you can find relatives on Facebook, connect with and keep up with family, build your family tree, and share family news and photos. The application sits in the left sidebar, and family members are listed in a box that is similar to the Friend box situated directly above it.

   b. Mundia by Mundia is another family tree application. It allows you to build a family tree and share it with others, contact other members, discover new relatives, and share family information and pictures. According to the Facebook page for Mundia, this application is available in 14 languages and linked into a global platform of more than 12 million trees and 1.25 billion profiles. So it is a fun way to link up with family, known and unknown, all over the world.

9. Sandra can also use the many photo sharing and display apps, like the Slide Show apps already mentioned to show and share family pictures with her family members. If she enters an application search for "photo sharing," many, many application possibilities appear for photo sharing, photologging, editing, and displaying.

By now, Sandra has a very full and dynamic Facebook presentation that screams out how she likes to spend her time and what she is about. This is all positive action and ingenuity. A college admissions visitor will be pleased with all that Sandra has going on with her business, creativity, charitable causes, and family life. This is as it should be.

Sandra's application options are just a small sampling of what is available on Facebook. MySpace has its own universe of applications. Whether you are parked at Facebook or MySpace, a little research will yield a cornucopia of choices suitable for your areas of interest and endeavor.

Though the effort expended creating a full Facebook presence may seem daunting, it may not require any more time than you are already spending online. You may just need to redirect your online activity to this kind of creative effort until you feel you have created a positive representation of yourself for your college application process. The time will be well worth the effort.

Use Your Web Site or Blog to Showcase Your Talents

Use Your Web Site or Blog to Showcase Your Talents

Blogging has become a very popular medium for young people to express themselves online.

Fundamentally, a blog (or web log) is a Web site that is dedicated to online journaling. That is, the blog site is updated periodically with content (or writing) by a person or a group of people. The entry, more commonly called a post, can be accompanied by images and links to Internet destinations. The blog format is an ideal medium for a writer or aspiring writer because it is as unstructured as a blank piece of paper. And yet, it provides a dated format, lots of ways to enhance your compositions, and the promise of a potential audience.

Now that blogging has become so popular (with 12 million people doing it in the U.S. alone), blogging has evolved into its own art form. The great news is, unlike most things that become hugely popular, blogging (for the most part) is still free. Hosting services, like Blogger, Wordpress, and Typepad, allow you to establish a site in minutes. All you need is an email address. And the hosting services offer a variety of templates and widgets, so that your site can be customized to your liking.

You can use your site as a personal journal where everything that you are doing and creating is chronicled and displayed. Or you can develop a specialty blog to showcase a particular interest or talent. However you fashion your site, you can create an inviting, engaging, and dynamic place that, when found by an admissions officer (or anyone for that matter), speaks volumes about who you are and what you do well. Below are seven great things you can do with blogs.

– 12 –
Unleash the Writer

Personal Blogs: The vast majority of teen and young adult blogs are formatted as online journals and are dedicated to the thoughts and day-to-day happenings in the lives of the writers. They tend to be very personal in nature and very casual in prose. A personal blog's subject matter can be absolutely anything—your daily life, your friends, even your college application process. Lots of bloggers use their site to chronicle an event, transition, or project, such as planning a trip, a weight loss diet, or marathon training. These blogs usually cover a finite period of time and have a distinct beginning and end. When you want to showcase your writing skills, make sure you choose a subject that will keep you motivated to write frequently and well ("well" meaning you are willing to edit carefully). Your posts can be as short or long as you desire, but they should be well planned and executed. You do not need to say something profound or even meaningful with each post. You just need to say it in your best prose, using complete words and not IM speak (an LOL sprinkled in here or there is not so bad). These writing rules apply to any blog that you want to put forth as a potential collection of writing samples. After all, as a writer, no matter what the subject of the blog, each post is a sample of what you can do.

If you want to see samples of blogs that are acceptable to admissions offices, look at the student blogs that are featured on the school's admissions sites. Even though these are student blogs, the admissions offices would not likely use them for admissions purposes without some guidelines and approval from the admissions personnel. When you read these blogs, notice that they avoid profanity and slang. The bloggers are able to express themselves with interest and uniqueness without relying on word bombs. This is how you should approach your own posts when you are writing with a potential admissions visitor in mind.

If you'd like to see examples of other student blogs, go to http://www.teenblogs.com. This is a portal which lists teen and student blogs by state. It's an exhaustive list of teen, young adult, and college student blogs.

Fiction Blogs: If you are more of a fiction writer, you may be interested in starting a fiction blog. You may already have a collection of short stories that you can post. Or if you want to create one or a series of stories, you can post them in whole or in installments on your blog. Enhance your posts with your own pictures or pictures from a stock photo site, and you have the makings of an online fiction destination. Keep in mind that the Internet reading experience is different from print. Usually an online audience prefers shorter stories or stories broken up into chapters.

Fictional Blogs: Another popular way to write fiction online is by creating a blog that is written by a fictional character. Fictional blogs are written, usually in real time, in the voice of a personality you make up. These blogs are often used by fiction writers as either a springboard for a novel or as a stand-alone work. If you choose this route, you should disclose somewhere prominent on your site that the content is fictional. This format allows you a little more freedom to express yourself. You can explore somewhat controversial topics that you might not comfortably discuss on your personal blog. Your fictional character does not have to be a person. One blogger spoke through the voice of her dog, another through the ghost of a long deceased relative. You can find examples of fictional blogs and articles about how to successfully do them at http://www.blogfiction.org.

As with all fiction writing, some planning is advisable. You can just write as you go, but a sound piece of fiction has good character development and at least a central plot and a main outline. But feel free to let your imagination and creativity take flight.

Poetry Blogs: Are you a poet? Do you have notebooks full of your poetry and nowhere to share them? Perhaps you could create a blog that posts a poem a day. Or you could devise a blog where you experiment with different types of poetry. Monday could be haiku day and Friday could be sonnets day. Poetry blogs are very popular. They are many and quite diverse, both professional and amateur. There are lots of teen and young bloggers, too. The great thing about blogging is that you don't have to worry about market saturation. There can never be too many poetry blogs. In the blogging world, it is customary for bloggers of a certain genre to support, link to, and network with each other. So the more you read other poetry blogs and make comments on the content, the more you, too, will be read by your poetic contemporaries. This is true for every kind of blogging. Communities form around interests and niches and soon you have created a following and a circle of like-minded bloggers. For a listing of poetry blogs, start at http://poetryblogrankings.com/default.aspx, which is a ranked database of poetry bloggers. Their Top 100 Poetry Blogs list will provide plenty of diverse examples of successful online poets.

You can also create a blog that features, discusses, and invites the inclusion of poetry from others. Even though this kind of blog would not carry your own poetry, you could include your reviews, discussions, and critiques of other poems. Your writing would still be showcased, as well as your organizational, critical thinking, and editing skills. To see an example of this type of poetry blog, you can explore http://thebesta-mericanpoetry.typepad.com/ and http://www.world-classpoetryblog.com/.

Novel Blogs (and other projects): A novel blog is a site where an author chronicles the writing of a novel. This is another example of a project blog briefly discussed earlier in this chapter. If you are working on a novel, you can blog about the process. You can discuss the different literary aspects of your writing journey—how you have devised the plot or where your characters come from. You can take the reader along as the actual story unfolds. Or you can discuss the difficulty of sticking to your writing schedule and what you do to get past writer's block. The novel blog is a tool writers use to cultivate an audience for the eventual book, once it is completed. It is an especially rewarding project if you enjoy the writing process and want to extol the joys of the creative process. As with many project blogs, you can give yourself a set starting date and a projected completion date, so that you challenge yourself to finish the novel. In this way, your readers can support you and encourage you to keep going. They become invested in the endeavor. The most famous project blog to date is the one immortalized in the best-selling book and motion picture, *Julie and Julia.* This is a true story about how blogger Julie Powell endeavored to cook her way through *Mastering the Art of French Cooking,* by famous chef Julia Child. Powell blogs about the trials and tribulations she experiences while attempting all 524 recipes in Child's monolithic cookbook. She gives herself one year to complete the recipes. You can use this model for writing a novel or any number of other projects or goals. The key is to set a timetable and deadline for yourself. Even if you don't make it, you have created urgency and drama, motivating your readers to come back and see how you are doing.

Blogs are a medium of the written word. So really, any subject of focus will provide opportunity to showcase your writing talent and commitment. And speaking of commitment, as you have probably already gathered, blogs can take a considerable amount of time to maintain. Lots of writers have begun blogs only to run out of steam after a short while. If you are fortunate to already have a body of work that you can post, you are way ahead of the game. So think about what you have already written. Do you have good compositions from school that you can polish up and post? Do you have volumes of journals that you would be willing to share? These will be your simplest way to start.

– 13 –

Unleash the Artist

If you are a prolific artist—and if you are already participating in social media—you likely already know that there is not just a thriving art world online, but there is a thriving art universe. The Internet is a visual realm that offers many ways to house, exhibit, and sell your art. If you are applying to an art school or the art department of a liberal arts college, your portfolio is a very important part of your application. Many schools allow you to submit your work through a link to an online destination, as opposed to sending a compact disc or DVD. The portfolio submission requirements are very specific and usually have a strict deadline that is earlier than the general application deadline. Artists pursuing this avenue of admissions should connect with the school as soon as possible in their process to get the details ironed out and addressed.

But if you are an artist or art lover who wants to showcase your work or knowledge of art as part of the general application process, the following suggestions are geared for you.

There are art blogs and there are art Web sites. Blogs are usually free (or at least you can create a very good blog site at no cost). Web sites cost money at the very outset. For a Web site, you have to determine and purchase a domain name (or a .com) and then you must pay a hosting service for your Web site. The truth is, now that services are available to enable a nontechnical person to create his own site, sites that can be created with a blogging service and a Web site are very close to merging—with very little difference between them. But the more features and functionality of a traditional Web site that you require (like additional pages or shopping cart purchasing services), you will likely have to pay for them whether you choose a blog or a Web site service.

If you want to keep things simple, choose a free blogging host. Most of them offer beautiful templates with which you can upload pictures of your art and display it in creative and aesthetically pleasing ways. For an art blog, you do not necessarily need written posts, though filling out the "About Me" section is a good idea. Even if you do not want many words, you should put your name in a number of locations on your site so that if someone (such as a college admissions staff member) happens to search your name in a search engine, your site will be listed high in the search results. For this purpose, you might even put your name in the title of the blog, like this: "Picture Houston: The Photography of Gina Carroll." You should include your name in the "About Me" section and perhaps in some of the picture captions. The blogging services—Blogger, Wordpress, and Typepad— offer some wonderful art and photography templates. Web site creation sites like Weebly.com and Wix.com also allow you to create a Web site for many different functions, including art, photography, and design.

You can create your site for free and they will host for free, but if you need a domain or you want to move your design to another site, there are charges.

Populating and updating your site with good quality photos is a vital part of a good art blog. As a digital native, you are fortunate to have very easy and inexpensive ways to take and manipulate photographs. With your phone, digital still, or video camera, you can take and download your photographs, adding your works as you create them.

ArtistsWhoBlog.com is a site that features artist bloggers. The site has interviews and a long link list of art blogs. This is a great place to see what artists are doing online and read about their lives and motivations. Artbloggin.com is an art blog directory, where you will find hundreds of beautiful sites that should inform and inspire you with the different ways the art blog medium is used by creative folks. For a simple portfolio Web site, look at http://marybrossman.weebly.com, created by teen artist Mary Brossman. Her site features her drawings, paintings, sculptures and installations, short films, and her biography, each on a separate page.

So whether you decide to display your art with or without commentary, or with a chronicle of your progress, your art site can be a beautiful place to entertain college admissions officers you are trying to impress. Chapter 19 discusses ways to connect your different social media, so that if an admissions visitor finds you in one place online, you can send them to your other showcase destinations.

– 14 –

Unleash the Enthusiast

There are some things that you like to do and there are some things that you like to admire and enjoy as an observer, fan, or promoter. Chapter 12 discusses the poetry blogs that feature and discuss the poetry of others. Chapter 13 discusses a blog that champions the works of other artists and their blogs. These are just two examples of blogs and Web sites that focus on the works of others. There are countless other kinds of enthusiast blogs—sites that highlight an area of passion that may include your own activity, an enthusiastic community, and the other individuals who also love and honor your interest.

Favorite Cause: You can start a blog that brings focus to a cause or charity. If you are involved or beginning a social cause or charitable effort, blog about it.

Blogging is a great way to explain what you are doing and chronicle your progress. A blog or Web site is also a handy promotional tool for volunteer or charitable efforts. If you want to send out an email blast (or announcement to a large group of your friends) about your volunteer project, community service activity, or charitable drive, you can keep your email short by giving a quick explanation of your project and then including a link to your blog or Web site. In this way, you have provided a place to go for details and contact information. A blog or Web site can also act as a hub for all of your other social media tools. Even if you have utilized Facebook to send announcements and status updates about your effort, and perhaps Twitter (the micro-blogging site) to engage conversations about your project, the blog or Web site can be a place where your longer and more detailed written content is housed.

YouthNoise.com is a good location to find a nice sampling of teen blogs about community service and social causes. This is a social networking site where kids can get involved in causes and showcase their own projects. You can read the many blogs that are on the site. You can join the site and blog yourself. Youth Noise also offers their MyCause tool, which allows you to create personalized Web pages for your cause. Colleges love to see applicants who are really involved in community service. Now that many high schools require community service hours toward graduation, students who choose to devote considerable time and effort to causes that are truly meaningful to them need to separate themselves from the high school herd of obligatory do-gooders. A dedicated Web site or blog is a useful way to record and highlight the time you've spent on your charity and the differences you've made.

Here are a handful of other kinds of enthusiast sites, but the possibilities are endless.

Fan site: If you love something enough to dedicate your time and energy to learning more about it, chances are there is someone else out in the blogsphere who does too. Create an interactive Web site or a blog devoted to the object of your admiration—a celebrity, sports personality, author, and so forth. This site is a way to showcase your writing, your Internet prowess, and your organizational skills if you are cultivating and engaging a reader base.

Hollywoodteentalk.blogspot.com is an example of a teen gossip site. If you choose to create a site that discusses celebrities in the gossip format, it is best to follow this blog's example and keep your material positive and upbeat.

MadgeTribe.blogspot.com is one of the many unofficial Madonna fan sites. The blog has a forum page where fans can discuss the latest news concerning their favorite pop star. The forum feature was added to the site through a link to Forumotion.com, which is a forum hosting service. The service is free of charge. Like MadgeTribe.com, you can simply create the forum and then add the link to your blog site. Chapter 15 discusses other ways to create communities of common interest through forums.

The JustinBieberShrine.blogspot.com site was

created by a Canadian fan, who professes to be constantly adding new bells and whistles to this blog. It is already chock-full of features. Oh the time dedicated fans are willing to invest in their online celebrity "shrines"! If this is your interest, make your time count with a tribute that is uplifting and uniquely expressed.

Book Review Site: If you are a bibliophile and find that reading is your favorite pastime, and if you devour books by the week or maybe even by the day, you should consider creating a book review blog. Since you are already doing the reading, all you have to do is critique the book—say what you loved, liked, and did not like about your favorite author, genre, or book series. If you discuss authors you like, for example, you can post videos of interviews or book previews that may be available on YouTube. (Chapter 17 will discuss creating and using video on your site.) Here are some great examples of teen and young adult book review sites:

- TeenBookReview.wordpress.com
- AllFiveStars.blogspot.com
- MrsMagooReads.com
- AndAnotherBookRead.blogspot.com
- EmsBookShelf.com
- Fashion Blog: Parlay your love of fashion and shopping into a blog. Fourteen-year-old Weronika Zalazinska from Krakow, Poland, has created a well-regarded fashion blog, RasberryandRed.blogspot.com. (She was featured in TeenVogue.com in June 2010 as the "Blogger-of-the-Moment.") She combines her unique style with great photographs to create an engaging site. Also, KarlasCloset.blogspot.com relies heavily on photographs to create an aesthetically appealing destination. Fashion blogs are very popular and often quickly develop a fan base of readers. Online magazine enthusiasts are finding that fashion blogs are great low-cost alternatives to printed periodicals.
- Television Blog: There are blogs dedicated to

one favorite television show or all things related to TV. These two sites have the full spectrum of television programming covered: We Like TV Blog at www.jenmira.blogspot.com and Televisionaryblog.com.

With an enthusiast site you can provide all of the written content or you can borrow (with permission, of course) or solicit contributions from other enthusiasts who are involved in or already writing about the subject. As you may have surmised, it takes more than a passion to blog about your subject in the extensive way that these fans and devotees have. A blog requires commitment, but your blogging commitment does not have to be long-term. You may decide to set up a blog to showcase your interests and talents just for your college application.

− 15 −
Connect with Like-minded People

Another online avenue for pursuing your interests is to join established groups of people who are interested in the same pursuits. Ning.com is a popular platform for joining or creating your own social network site. Each of the hundreds of Ning.com sites is centered on a special interest. This is a whole universe of enthusiasts who come together and converse on forums, blog, share photos and videos, chat, take polls, and more. Crimespace, for example, is a network for readers and writers of crime fiction. If you are interested in crime fiction, instead of, or in addition to, creating your own blog site, you can join this network of 2,000 members (as of this writing) and post your content here.

When you join a Ning group you register and create a profile. Your profile is your own personal page on the network, where you share your personal information and express your interest. You can add links to your blog or Web site on this profile, or you can blog right from your profile page. There are greater limitations to how you can personalize your profile, but once you are registered, you can take part in all of the activities of the group. Often, bloggers will join a Ning group in order to promote their own blog and let others know where they are writing about the subject. There is a charge for creating a group on Ning. There is no charge for participating as a member.

There are also Web sites (versus networks) that you can join as a member. For example, YouthNoise.com (discussed in Chapter 14) is a network site for teens who are interested in social causes. In addition to blogging, YouthNoise offers a very interactive platform to participate in community service and charitable efforts. Whether you have a cause that you are promoting or you are looking for a way to get involved, YouthNoise.com offers opportunities to make yourself and your interests known.

Fanpop.com is a social media network of fan sites. Users can create a fan page for any topic of interest. The page is maintained by the community of fans. On Fanpop.com you can join a fan club or create one. The clubs are very interactive—each fan page can include videos, links, image galleries, and forums—and on each fan club page there is a list of all the other fan members.

A word about Forums and chat rooms: Before there were social networks and before there were blogs, there were forums and chat rooms. Forums started out as very simple places to go online and join a running conversation on a topic. They were the first medium that allowed people to sign on anonymously and share. Anonymity was a very popular feature and caused forums and chat rooms to rapidly proliferate across the Internet. Social networks soon replaced forums and chats in popularity because networks offer so much more in the way of functionality, but these simple forum and chat models did not disappear. They just no longer stand alone as a destination. More commonly, they are tied to a social network or Web site page as an added feature and a chance to keep a topical discussion going. Some Web site host services offer the option of adding a forum to your site. There are also forum hosting sites that allow you to create a forum on their site. In this way, you can link the forum to your site. Many of these forum hosting services are free of charge. Adding a forum to your site is a way to transform your site from a very static medium to a much more dynamic and interactive one.

These online communities are a rewarding way to pursue your interests, because by connecting you with other enthusiasts, your knowledge and exposure to your interest grow and deepen. The more that like-minded people pool their knowledge and resources, the greater each person's experience is enhanced. When you direct a college admissions officer to your networked special interest sites, they can see how you interact with others and how deeply you are involved in your work, hobby, or passion.

Be warned, however. Forums and chat rooms can

be dangerous places, especially for teens. Because most participants are anonymous and the medium is less restricted with regard to membership and security, forums and chat rooms are known to attract online predators, bullies, and stalkers. Choose your forums carefully and **never** disclose your identity or your location on these sites. If you create a forum on your own site, make sure you report any suspicious behavior or participants to your parents and your site administrators. For more information about safety, see Appendix 1: A Word About Safety.

– 16 –
Show Your Business Side

D o you have a business? Are you involved in a money-making venture? If so, your college choices should definitely know about it. Colleges look favorably upon applicants who are enterprising. The entrepreneur represents a trailblazer, an intellectual risk-taker, and a hard worker. These are very desirable traits in a college prospect. Traditionally, you have two ways to tell college admissions about your business enterprise: on the short answer and essay parts of your application and during an interview. But with social media, you can use online places to tell your business story. As a digital native, you know that a business does not exist unless it exists online. Even businesses whose focuses have nothing to do with computers or the Internet must often use the Internet to market their goods and services. You can talk about your enterprise until you are blue in the face, but if a person cannot quickly find your company name online using a search engine, your talk is for naught.

A business site should be very much like the enthusiast sites discussed earlier—the only difference being that the time an enthusiast invests in finding readers and other devotees is time an entrepreneur invests in finding customers. There are endless and wonderful ways to display and promote your business online. No matter how small and fledgling it may be, your money-making venture can command a big Internet presence.

A discussion of how to set up a business Web site is beyond the scope of this book. Plenty of reliable online and offline sources can teach you the basics of creating and promoting your business on the Internet through a visit to your local library or a search or two online. If you want to see what other teen business-people are doing, try TeenBusinessForum.com and TeenOnlineEntrepreneur.com. These blog sites are headed by teens and provide lots of start-up and Internet business insights and advice.

There are also networked sites that allow you to sell your products in a marketplace. These sites, like Etsy.com, allow you to join a community of buyers and sellers, and to set up shop easily. At Etsy.com, when you sign up as a seller, you are able to set up your own shop by customizing a banner, filling out a profile, and setting your shop policies. The community functions allow you to interact with other sellers and buyers through forums and chat rooms. They have organized groups called Teams, by which members come together to network and share skills and resources in order to promote their shops. Etsy is not a free service. You pay to list your sale items.

The key, for college admissions purposes, is that you make your business known to the colleges with whom you are applying. If you have a tiny enterprise, you should at least set up a one-page introduction blog site that includes your contact information and the details of what you are selling. This permits you to refer to your business on your other media and send visitors to your site for more information. When a college lands on your Facebook page, they should find your discussion of your business there, which will intrigue them enough to click through to your site and see how enterprising you are. Chapter 18 discusses how you can integrate your media so that visitors can find all of your online destinations.

Make a Statement with Video

Almost all of the media discussed thus far can incorporate video. You can add video to your web and blog sites and to your Facebook and other social networking pages. Video is a very popular way to communicate your ideas. The popularity of You-Tube.com speaks to the power of video to entertain and inform. We have become, after all, a generation of watchers. Even college admissions personnel, who try to keep the amount of information input from applicants to a minimum, have begun to embrace video as an acceptable addition to the usual written submissions. Some colleges, like Tufts University, St. Mary's College, and George Mason University, now officially accept videos as application supplements. The Common Application has accepted video as part of its arts supplement since 2008. With the encouragement of these universities, the potential of video for admissions has significantly expanded. Already, it's clear that video submissions have had a very favorable impact on admissions officers.

Andrew Flagel, Dean of Admissions and Associate Vice President of Enrollment Development for George Mason University, says in his article "Yes or No to Video with Your College Application": "In 20 years in admissions, I have reviewed some wonderful, but far more truly awful, written essays. However, the handful of videos I have reviewed have been thoughtful and insightful."[1]

Lee Coffin, Tuft's dean of undergraduate admissions, told the *New York Times* that he got the idea of soliciting videos from applicants after watching an impressive video someone sent to him. "I thought, 'If this kid applied to Tufts, I'd admit him in a minute, without anything else,'" Coffin said.[2] Coffin feels that video offers a glimpse of a prospect that is more complete, genuine, and "completely transparent."

The great advantage of video is that the possibilities are wide open. Admissions offices are interested in how students express themselves, and not so much in their technical skills. Yes, some kids turn in technologically advanced video productions. But many submit creative and interesting videos filmed on simple and relatively inexpensive camcorders (like the Flip video camera), and on the tool that just about every teen possesses (or at least has access to), the cell phone camera. Some students talk about themselves or hold interviews with imaginary admissions officers. Some perform original plays, dances, and scientific demonstrations.

Tufts allows you to upload your video onto You-Tube and then submit the URL (or your videos Internet address) to the school, so that they can find it online. In this way, Tufts admissions shows that they are ahead of the social media curve. But other schools' admissions offices are catching on fast. And since schools are beginning to look upon video so favorably, it makes sense to give video some serious consideration. This medium is no longer only for artists and aspiring filmmakers. Anyone doing something interesting and well, should consider submitting an application video. Even if the schools you are applying to do not formally accept video as part of the application, you may be able to catch their interest in your videos by putting the videos online.

In the five years of YouTube's existence, it has become and remained the go-to place for uploading and viewing video. On YouTube, like your other social media sites, you can join and create your own channel. Then, in addition to uploading your own video, you can create playlists of videos from others and send messages to and share videos with other YouTube users. When you upload your video onto your channel, the video is given a URL number and an embed code. You can use these at your other sites online—Facebook and your blog—to either link to your video or to embed your video right onto your other sites. YouTube also allows you to connect your YouTube channel directly with your

Facebook account, for easy sharing.

If you decide that you want your YouTube channel to be its own destination, you can customize your YouTube profile with your personal information, including links to your Web sites. The YouTube profile has as much detail potential as your Facebook pages. So this is another place a school can learn more about you. The settings also allow your channel to spotlight certain videos and show your recent activity. You can also download a profile picture. When you link an admissions officer to your application video, you are linking them to another portal into your online world.

Though YouTube is the most popular video platform online, there are other easily accessible Web sites. Flickr.com, Yahoo's photo management site, also allows you to upload, store, and share video. Note, however, this site has a 90-second time limit on video duration. You can upload a longer video, but only the first 90 seconds will show. Similar sites are TinyPic.com, DropShots.com, and photobucket.com. Viddler.com is solely a video sharing site. It gives you easy ways to customize the video player and link it to your other locations online, like your Web or blog site. These sites are free for basic service, with fees for upgrades.

Here are a few suggestions for optimizing your application video:

1. Your application video should, like all of your media, highlight that special thing you love or have mastered. Remember college admissions are most interested (other than in your grades, of course) in the activities that you feel passionate about and have committed some time and effort to.

2. You can film your video in any way you desire to get your message across. Your video might feature your conversation directly to the camera from your messy bedroom or it might be an animated version of yourself. You might decide not to feature yourself at all. Instead, you could submit a video of a production for which you

were the writer, director, or set builder.

3. Your video should not be long (Tufts requires a maximum of one minute. The Common Application's arts supplement allows 10 minutes).

4. Music greatly enhances videos. There are a number of places online where you can get music without violating copyright laws. If you choose to use YouTube, use their AudioSwap feature. The three following sites offer royalty-free music, meaning you can use it without violating copyright laws as long as you give the artist credit on your video or site: Incompetech.com, audionautix.com, and jamendo.com. Incompetech.com and audionautix.com offer instrumental music. Jamendo.com offers vocals. The music on these sites is free.

5. Simple is good. You do not need expensive video and computer equipment. Colleges are interested in seeing who you are and what makes you special. They are not interested in a slick production. But if you are a technological

whizz and that is what you want to highlight through your video, go for it!

A Word About Vlogging

Another effective use of video is by creating a vlog. A vlog is a video blog. If you like to express yourself through video instead of the written word, you can set up a regular blog site and embed your own video presentations instead of written posts. Or you can do your vlogging right from your YouTube channel. Or both. Some bloggers do a combination of blogging and vlogging on their sites. Again, with the video medium, your options for topic and format are wide open. Some vloggers talk about the goings-on in their lives as a one-on-one conversation with the camera. Some folks produce topical series on a particular subject, like a how-to cooking series, while others do interviews and man-on-the-street pedestrian interactions. Vlogging adds another dimension to your site. It is more interactive, dynamic, and engaging.

You have the opportunity to show more of yourself and your personality. Readers and viewers feel like they've had a conversation. Since many admissions directors have expressed an affinity to video presentations, your blog-vlog can be a way to offer more video than the one-minute application video by linking all of your online destinations together and directing your admissions visitors to your video site. How to do this is discussed in the next chapter.

– 18 –
Integrate Your Media

If you have decided to go all out on your social media, then you have several places you can be found online. Admissions directors make it very clear that they do not spend their precious time stalking around the Internet for every candidate. Daniel Parish, director of admissions at Dartmouth, said that his office (and he suspects most other schools) do not have the manpower to check out every applicant online: "The number of our staff has declined and the number of applicants has doubled. So we just don't have the time or the inclination to do a search for each person." This sentiment is echoed throughout the college admissions community. And yet, some officers admit to the ease of finding an applicant on Facebook and seeing their page on a computer screen while reviewing their application. "Finding an applicant is quick and looking over a Facebook page is an efficient way to see what the applicant is about," said one admissions officer who preferred not to be identified. Currently, it is unclear the extent to which your online social pages, Web sites, and blogs will be seen by the admissions folks you'd like to send there. Your chances will vary depending on the school and its admissions policies. Your best bet is to make sure that if they do find you, they find your best self-representation, and that once they are on one of your social media pages, they will be motivated and inspired to link to your others.

The steps to link your social media are easy. Most social media sites facilitate this because links are a great way to increase connections with other users. Take advantage of link opportunities to connect all of your information. Since Facebook is currently the most utilized destination among college admissions personnel, let all of your roads lead to Facebook. Facebook makes it easy to load your page with all of the content from your other sites.

To do this, follow these steps:

Step 1: Connect all of your college review site profiles to your Facebook profile, if they offer that function. Many of the college review sites offer this connection—CampusBuddy, Communiversity, StuVu, and Unigo, to name a few.

Step 2: Use the RSS Feed function on Facebook to stream the content of your Web site and blog. In this way, your Facebook page will show your blog posts and videos right on the page. Go to http://www.face-book.com/apps/directory.php and type in RSS Feed into the search window. Several choices of applications are available that bring your blog posts to your Facebook page. Peruse them to find which one suits you best. One very popular RSS Feed application is through NetworkedBlogs. With the NetworkedBlogs application, you can choose to have your blog posts appear under a separate tab on your Facebook profile. The tab will say "Blog." So your visitors can just click the tab and read a listing of your blog posts. If you include pictures on your posts, a thumbnail of the picture will also appear next to the blog post listing. Now your visitors do not have to click away from your Facebook page to see your Web sites, blogs, and videos.

Step 3: For YouTube, in the Facebook applications directory, you can also find applications that allow a YouTube page and tab on your Facebook profile. Your videos from your channel will show up right on your Facebook page. No need to travel. There are currently two applications that achieve this:

YouTube Channel by Timert.me and YouTube by Mohammed Asif. Both of these apps can be found in the applications directory and can make your Face-book profile a YouTube one-stop shop.

If an admissions officer finds your other sites first, you also must make sure you direct them to your Facebook page. If, for example, you have submitted a video with your application, you might provide the URL to the video's YouTube location. Once admissions visitors have clicked onto YouTube to view your video, they may notice that you have a channel. Suppose they like your video so much that they want to see what else you've done. (No admissions personnel will admit that they do this kind of expansive exploring of a candidate, but we all know what happens when you find something different and intriguing online. You keep clicking to see more.) So now they are on your channel and can view your profile. Your profile can include the URL to your Web site or blog. You can also put your Facebook URL in that section, or you can include your URLs in the "About Me" section. Take full advantage of the "About Me" section to list your other locations. If you have loaded all of your information and online locations onto your Facebook page as suggested, you should highlight your Facebook URL in as many locations on your YouTube channel page as possible. Once they land on your Facebook page, they need go no farther. Three key places to put the Facebook URL link are: On the "Info" section for your application video and on the "Web site" and "About Me" sections of your YouTube profile. Do not load your "About Me" section with too much other information or your visitors may miss the link. Perhaps your "About Me" section can simply read: "You can find out everything about me on Facebook" and include the link. This teaser should do the trick.

If the admissions officer lands on your Web site or blog first, make sure you have embedded Facebook links and YouTube links on the sidebar of the site so that they know you also reside in those places. Again, if your Facebook is loaded, highlight that link the most.

Now that all of your online information is linked and integrated, the most important thing to do is make sure all of that information is positive and appropriate and only reflective of your highest self.

The Online Makeover

The Online Makeover

You already know that colleges do not yet visit the social media pages of every applicant. But what you may not know is that there is one instance when they are almost certain to check things out, and that is when they receive information that a prospect's page reflects poorly on them. Universities and colleges want to admit students who will contribute to, and not detract from, the school community. They are deeply invested in making sure the entering class will perform well academically and fit in well with the current students. Unigo.com and WSJ OnCampus held a webcast in 2009 that addressed the use of social media in the admissions process. The college admissions panelists expressed a consensus that their primary reason for going online to investigate an applicant

146

was concern for the school community. Eric J. Furda, Director of Admissions at the University of Pennsylvania, said, "Community well-being is critically important to us." Roby Blust, Dean of Admissions and Enrollment Planning at Marquette, agreed: "People take it very seriously being a part of that community." Blust stated that most of the information admissions offices receive about student activity online is from the greater community.[1] This interest in protecting the community is why you, as an applicant, put yourself at risk with compromising social media content during the applications process and even after you have been admitted. A recent survey of admissions offices cited in the Unigo-WSJ College webcast, stated that of all the admittances that are rescinded, nearly 7 percent were based on "inappropriate postings on a Web site after [the students] were already admitted."

You might ask, from whom would an admissions office receive a tip about negative social media information about you? Take a moment to consider who, during your application process period, might be looking at your Facebook page. In addition to admissions personnel, you may attract:

- Teachers writing your letters of recommendation
- Scholarship committee members
- Potential employers
- Your friends
- Friends of friends
- Classmates who are not friends
- Fellow Applicants

In addition to this list of potential visitors, add anyone looking over the shoulders of the people on this list as they peruse your information. Now, of all of these people, some may be alumni or current students of the schools to which you are applying. And some may be competitors.

Now consider who might be looking at your pages after you are admitted to the college of your dreams:

- Your academic advisor
- University staff for dorm and roommate decisions
- Your resident advisor
- Your professors
- Employers, including for Work-Study consideration

The potential for your pages to be viewed by an interested member of a college community increases as the number of your social media friends increases. Even if you have gone through the steps to create your optimal online presence by loading your social media pages with positive information, you still need to do a clean sweep of potentially harmful content put there by you and also by others. Then you must visit your pages often and manage them so that no new dangers arrive.

– 19 –

Control Where Your Content Goes and Who Sees It

When you choose to share your personal information online, you should still be very careful and deliberate about who you want to find you and see the different components of your sites. If you have been a member of Facebook for more than one year, you may not be aware that the site has undergone several generations of privacy changes recently. These changes have resulted in several shifts in the amount of information accessible to others outside of the people on your friend list. Now is a very good time to review your privacy settings.

Facebook's new privacy settings (which just rolled out June 2010) allow you to set privacy levels for every component of your page in a much more simplified fashion. In the top right corner of your page, you can find your privacy settings in the drop-down menu under the Account tab. On the new privacy settings page, you will find:

Basic Directory: Starting with "Basic Directory," you can control how you are found in the Facebook directory. The Basic Directory default setting allows everyone to see all of the information housed under this heading. If you do nothing to adjust your Basic Directory privacy settings, all of that information will be available to all other Facebook users. But if you wish to invoke some limitations, you can now even restrict disclosure of your friend list and your "Pages" (formerly "Fan Pages") for better privacy control. If you want to restrict strangers or unknown visitors from finding you, you can set each category to "Friends Only." The only item you must share with everyone is your profile picture.

Sharing on Facebook: This section allows you to determine the privacy settings for all of the informational categories on your page. You can restrict access to your posts, pictures, comments, and personal information. The menu gives you four templates that allow you to set all of your settings basically to one designated level—either "Everyone," "Friends of Friends," "Friends Only," or "Recommended." The "Recommended" template gives you settings that, according to the Facebook folks, allow access only by the people you approve. Their recommendations, however, reflect Facebook's interest in increasing your connections to others and not a focus on privacy. Even with a pro-growth agenda, the recommendations suggest that you restrict your personal location and contact information only to friends. As a fifth option, you can select a setting for each category under "Customize."

With regard to photographs, which are one of the difficult areas to control, you have two opportunities to gauge the privacy. You can restrict your status, photos, and posts with one setting. And you can restrict visitors from seeing the photos and videos that tag you. Here, you can set this choice so that only your friends can see photos and videos sent to your page by others. Since you do not know when these photos and videos may appear on your page, you may want a higher restriction on them. These pictures and videos may not meet your approval as you attempt to clean up your page for the college application process.

Again, you can and should restrict your address and telephone information. This point bears repeating because this level of privacy is very important to your safety. Facebook recommends that you restrict contact information to "friends only." However, it's far safer to remove this information from your page altogether. College admissions officers certainly will not be seeking this information from your social media sites.

Applications and Web sites: These settings are important because they address ways your information may end up on sites other than Facebook. There are lots of key settings here regarding games and other third-party applications. One concern with applications is that when your friends join another Facebook related Web site or app, quite a bit of your information may be accessible. You can now limit your exposure in this section. Similarly, the Instant Personalization setting allows you to limit how much a site can use your profile information to enhance the working of their site. This would apply, for example, to your college review sites since they use your Facebook profile information to fill in the profile on their sites. If you want to, you can limit access for that use.

And finally, you can decide what shows up on your public profile, the one that appears if someone searches for you using a search engine. This is how visitors who are not members of Facebook can find your Facebook page. If all of your information is open to everyone, they will see a summary of information on the abbreviated public profile, but then they can enter your page and see all the information that you've left open.

If you decide you do not want your page found by college admissions personnel, you should use the very highest privacy settings. You should start by restricting the public profile information so that you cannot be found by a search engine and the Basic Directory settings so that you will not be searchable within the Facebook site.

Block Lists: This section allows you to block certain people and applications from your page. If you know there are certain Facebook members who consistently make comments or tag you for pictures that compromise your page, you should unfriend them. But if you want to make sure that they cannot get to your information through shared friends, the next best step is to block them.

Getting a handle on your privacy setting options is important to controlling where your information goes and who sees it. But these settings are not infallible. You still must be very careful about what you are posting and sharing. Think long and hard about what you are adding to your pages, not just during your college application period, but always. A recent survey showed that 54 percent of social media users under 25 have posted something online that they later regret. This number is even higher for iPhone and Smart Phone users.[1] Nine percent of the regretful posters said that their unfortunate posts caused a relationship to end or trouble at work or home. You cannot control what your friends post on their own pages, but you can be extra careful, especially during this application period, to show restraint on your own posts. There are also ways to manage friends so that you can keep your page clean and still maintain a thriving social life on Facebook. Chapter 21 discusses how.

Clean House of Offensive Content and Photos

It's time to do the real clean-up work for your site. This is very important, especially if you have taken the steps to promote yourself on your online spaces. You have too much invested, and at stake, to let old discussions and photographs undermine your work and your college chances.

Starting with Facebook, go through your profile pages carefully and remove all content that can be viewed by admissions staff as compromising or inappropriate. It's important to make a distinction here between what you may feel is unacceptable content and what an admissions officer might find to be a poor reflection on you. You may not be aligned in your understanding of what offends admissions personnel. When asked what kind of social media content and behavior is objectionable to admissions personnel, some schools point to their honor code as a reliable measure. In fact, some admissions directors want their applicants to be aware of their school's honor code as they are applying. An honor code is a school's statement of expectation regarding academic integrity. They specifically address how students should conduct themselves during exams and with regard to graded work. Most codes, for example, prohibit students from receiving or giving assistance on exams and graded class work, from copying or allowing exam answers or work to be copied, and plagiarism. Basically, the honor code pertains to a student's honesty and self-restraint. In the spirit of the honor code, admissions officers are, as Janet Rapelye, Princeton's Admissions Director, states, "expecting at every step of the [admissions] process that [applicants] are working with a very highest level of integrity."

Many colleges post their honor codes online. You can find Princeton University's honor code here, www.princeton.edu/studentguide/academics_101/

honor_code/, and Stanford University's honor code here, www.stanford.edu/dept/vpsa/judicialaffairs/ guiding/honorcode.htm.

If a school finds that you have placed anything on your sites and pages that is dishonest, plagiarized, or misrepresentative of what you have actually accomplished, that school will likely not admit you. In addition, if your pages show evidence that you are behaving illegally, irresponsibly, or disrespectfully of others, a school may decide to pass you by. In light of this, take the following steps to remove any damaging information from all of your sites (especially Facebook):[1]

1. Remove any discussion about your alcohol-drinking habits and block any photographs where you appear to be drinking alcohol. Even if you are drinking legally and even if you are actually drinking root beer in a bottle that looks like a beer bottle, or apple juice in a wine glass, you should remove any appearance of alcohol

consumption.

2. Remove or block any photographs that show you or the people with you obviously under the influence.

3. Remove or block photographs with rude or suggestive gestures. If you would not do the gesture in front of your grandmother, remove it from your social media.

4. Remove any content that is cruel, abusive, or mean-spirited.

5. Unsubscribe from any groups or applications that show bias or bigotry. If you belong to a group called Old People Suck or I Hate Women Drivers or I Used to Kill the Hookers on Grand Theft Auto to Get My Money Back, what does that say about you? (Yes, unfortunately, these are actual Facebook Groups!)

6. Remove or block content or photographs that are sexually suggestive. Look at your pictures carefully, with the eye of a stranger. You may have some photographs that are innocent to the

people who were present when the photo was taken, but look inappropriate to someone who wasn't there.

7. Remove or block any content or photographs that admit to or portray illegal activity of any kind.

8. Unsubscribe from any groups that encourage illegal activity.

9. Remove or block any content or photographs that would make an admissions officer question your integrity, character, honesty, or judgment—even in the little things. For example, you should remove your detailed contact information like address and phone number. Since this puts you at a safety risk, it shows a failure to exercise good judgment.

10. Be aware of the captions under your photographs. The picture may be fine, but the caption or a comment under it may be profane or otherwise inappropriate.

Once you have removed all of the offending content and photographs, ask an adult to take a look at the page or site. Getting the perspective of an older person will be helpful. If you feel that your parent is too critical, agree to solicit help from another adult that you trust—a relative, teacher, college counselor, or school advisor.

Finally, social media pages and sites are very dynamic places. Your page will not remain unchanged after you've done all of your clean-up work. You will need to check it frequently to remove any photographs that appear from friends. You may just need to untag specific photographs, or you may decide to block pictures from certain friends altogether. The next chapter will discuss how to manage the information coming to your site or page from friends.

– 21 –
Carefully Manage Your "Friends"

Colleges understand that social media is all about connecting with and finding friends, old and new. Admissions personnel know that conversations between friends on Facebook are casual, personal, and yet expansive and ever-growing. Students on Facebook have huge numbers of friends. This combination of close and tangential relationships has forever changed the way the word "friend" is used. In light of this, schools know to take much of what is said on Facebook pages with a grain of salt. When admissions officers land on your Facebook page, they expect to see the friendly ribbing, relationship drama, and general angst that characterize your adolescent years. They expect to have to decipher your well-established use of acronyms and slang. And they know that they will encounter inside jokes and generational innuendo that will likely go right over their heads. These things are all fine and expected.

What they are most sensitive to and hoping not to find are clear demonstrations of poor judgment and character. Schools also know that you cannot control what your friends say and do, but your choice of friends and how you interact with them tell volumes about you.

With so many people connected and contributing to your Facebook page, it may seem overwhelming to try to control what might appear there at any given time. And you've worked too hard to cultivate the many friends and connections that you currently have to shut it all down in the name of college admissions.

There is a way to keep your social networking in place and still maintain a clean and positive place for your college admissions visitors to land. In order to be successful, you must carefully manage your friends. If you are finding that your friends are the wild cards of your Facebook clean-up effort, that their sometimes careless posts and controversial comments put you at risk, you can do two things. One is to limit their ability to contribute to your page. The other is to limit what others see of your friends' contributions.

An effective way to manage your friends is to divide them into lists. You can have a list or lists of friends who can have unlimited access to your page and others whom you want to restrict. You can create a list using the following steps:

1. On your Home Page, near the top of the left sidebar, click on "Friends."
2. Once you are on the Friends page, click the "Create a List" bar near the top right of the page.
3. The Lists window will pop up. You are prompted to type in a name. You can create any name for the list. None of your friends will know that they belong to one of your lists, nor will they be aware of any list name.
4. Populate the list by clicking on the profile pic-

ture of a friend or typing his or her name in the space provided. Group friends together whom you want to have the same privacy settings and access. You may have a list of "risky" friends made up of people who consistently add compromising content to your page.

Once you've made your lists, you can use them to quickly adjust your privacy settings. To limit the access of the people on your list of "risky friends," take the following steps:

1. Go to Privacy Settings, which is under the Account tab in the top right corner of your page. Under Sharing on Facebook, at the bottom of the box, click on "Customize Settings."
2. Under "Things Others Share," go to "Can Comment on posts." Scroll down the settings to "Customize" and in the top box choose "Specific People" and then type in the list name in the blank box.

3. Next, uncheck the box next to "Friends can post on my wall."

Now this list of friends cannot leave comments anywhere on your wall, and none of your friends can post on your wall. Though you cannot control from whom you receive tagged photos, you can restrict who sees tagged photos to "friends only," "specific people," or "only me."

You can also use lists for other groups whom you want to see only certain items on your page. If, for example, you are friends with your employer (not recommended) and fellow employees, you can put them on a list and restrict their access to certain information, like your photo galleries. This kind of restriction is less awkward than refusing to friend someone or blocking them from your page altogether.

If you are going to do a complete makeover of your page, you may want to post an update telling your friends what you are doing and why. You only need a short statement that says your page may look a little different because you are making changes for your college admissions process. Certainly your friends who are also planning to apply to colleges will understand and be looking to do the same. Many of these restrictions are not perceivable by your Facebook friends, so your friends will not know the degree to which you have limited their involvement in your Facebook page.

Even with all of the restrictions and limitations you place on your friends' activity, you should visit your page often and make sure nothing has landed on your page that is unwanted. If an unwanted photo appears on your wall because you have been tagged, you can remove it by viewing the picture and clicking the "Remove Tag" link next to your name. The picture will disappear and your name will be removed from the picture. You can also remove comments that show up on your wall by clicking the "Delete" located next to the comment.

The actions you take with regard to controlling

your friends' content to your page may seem very harsh compared with how you have been functioning on Facebook to this point. But remember you have a goal in mind—to get into the colleges of your choice. In all cases regarding your college admissions and your representation on Facebook, you are better safe than sorry.

Connect with Colleges—
Getting on Their Radar

Connect with Colleges—Getting on Their Radar

Previous chapters have discussed ways to connect with the colleges on your short list. You now know that colleges are interested in students who demonstrate interest in them, so part of your online social media effort should be to make real connections with schools. You want to send the message that, should you be accepted, you are likely to come. In furtherance of this, chapter 5 encouraged you to take a college tour, and chapter 6 discussed the value of participating in online college fairs and real-time virtual events. In addition, many colleges have embraced the social media format for their own official Web sites. In this way, you can go right to the source to get your questions answered and express your interest in an enhanced interactive experience.

— 22 —

Register on Official College Web Sites

Unlike the not-so-distant past when official college Web sites were static places that catered more to current students already on campus, many colleges have transformed their sites with all of the bells and whistles to attract and engage prospective students, and invite them to join their online communities. With a process very similar to other social media sites, you can register and obtain a log-in ID and a profile page where you are asked to input your personal information and your interests. Once you have registered, the school puts you on their mailing list so that you receive their information mailers and emails. Often your profile on the school Web site is a portal to inside information about the school and access to the school's application. For schools on your short list, registration on their site is a must. It tells the school that you are interested and gives you another direct connection with the admissions office.

University of Texas at Austin, for example, invites prospective students to join their community at bealonghorn.utexas.edu. Once you have registered, you are assigned an identification number that you keep throughout the process. When you fill out your personal information, you are given a page with five tabs, all designed to help you learn more about the university. You'll have a home page, where you can receive messages and updates on campus happenings, and a "Be a Longhorn" page that keeps you abreast of your application process. You are also assigned an admissions counselor at this time, whose contact link information is on the page, as well as important application dates. Once your application has been submitted, you are given a "mini status check" to remind you what has and has not been turned in. They also provide links to their academic and Student Life pages so that you can explore majors, read student profiles, and explore the "Longhorn Confidential" student blogs.

University of Southern California extends this kind of connection through their application process. Part One of their online application is a profile-like questionnaire that requests basic information about your location, high school, and interests. This alerts the university that you are interested in applying and gives you their first official point of contact. There is a separate deadline for this part of the application, but if you do not submit it, you can still apply without it by submitting Part Two of the application by a later deadline. According to their Web site, the university views Part One as "an optional way for prospective students to begin [their] process early."

College Web sites like the University of Texas' Be a Longhorn, and to some degree USC's Application Part One, are really designed to make applicants feel as though they are already a part of the school. Through these sites, the college is encouraging an exchange of information and communication that allows you and the school to get to know each other. If the official Web sites of the schools on your short list provide a profile registration process, take the following steps to optimize this important connection:

1. Register as soon as you can. Even if you are not sure if you'll apply to the school, register as soon as you are allowed. Many schools encourage juniors to register, but some schools do not have limitations. You can register with these schools as a high school freshman if you wish. The earlier you create your profile, the better— so that you can establish a longer-term commitment to that school as a serious pursuit.
2. Keep your contact information updated. Be easy to find. Schools often put you on their prospective student mailing lists from your profile information. This information is not a part of a network, but is confidential to the school only. College admissions offices are very serious about privacy and confidentiality.
3. Participate on the site. The University of Texas

site has an "Ask a Student" function, where you can chat with a student on the site. You can also ask the admissions office questions right from the Be a Longhorn page. And you can read current student, and even admissions counselor, profiles. The more you do "on record," the more you demonstrate your interest, and the more you will engage with the school community.

Not all schools offer this level of connection on their official Web sites, but they all have components that allow you to contact the admissions office, ask questions, request information, and schedule visits. You should use and participate in any interactive or communicative aspect of the site to the fullest extent applicable to your situation.

– 23 –
Friend and Follow Effectively (Social Media Etiquette)

Digital natives are not just using their social media sites for casual interaction. Recent studies show that students are increasingly turning to Facebook to take care of their school, work, and community responsibilities. They are interacting with their fellow students, co-workers, and teammates in order to initiate, plan, and coordinate projects, tasks, and events. It follows that if students are immersed in college admissions, they may think it a good idea to reach out to admissions officers on Facebook. In this way, students might surmise, they can show that they are earnestly interested in a certain school and in forging a relationship with admissions personnel. In fact, a 2009 survey conducted by Kaplan Test Prep and Admissions showed that students are doing just that. The

Kaplan researchers found that 70 percent of college admissions officials or someone in their offices has received Facebook or MySpace friend requests from applicants.[1]

When college admissions offices initially started using social media for outreach, many officers made themselves available to prospective students. But now that the colleges have instituted more formal ways for students to get and give information online, college admission offices uniformly frown upon students directly friending the personal Facebook pages of admissions staff. Trying to friend admissions officers or other personnel by way of their personal Facebook pages is a little like waiting in front of their homes and asking to come in. It makes an unfavorable impression and reflects poorly on a student's judgment and maturity. Most admissions officers have restricted their own Facebook accounts so that they are not easily found. Still, even if you find them, you are considered in bad form to attempt contact in this way. If you've met or communicated with an admissions officer, the best way to contact him is through email. Many high school–aged students feel that email is an antiquated form of communication, but for admissions personnel, it is still the preferred method. Email addresses are available on the colleges' official Web sites, either on the admissions pages or through the Web site faculty and staff directories.

As discussed in earlier chapters, colleges have several Facebook "Pages" (formerly called "Fan Pages") that offer you an alternative way to connect with the school. These Pages showcase their schools and the school's different departments, on-campus organizations, and activities. Princeton University has more than nineteen different Pages and Duke University has more than eighteen. You can connect to these pages by clicking the "I Like" icon on the Page. Then you will receive their status updates on your wall. And you can leave comments on their posts.

You can also join college affiliated Facebook groups like the Discover Dartmouth group, which is designed specifically for prospective students. You can post there and have your questions answered. You can also participate in a full array of topics on their discussion board.

It is vitally important to connect with the schools to which you are applying. You should use all of the avenues available online to get on their radars and express your interests, but you must use your best judgment and not be relentless or over-zealous. Colleges want students who are committed and tenacious, but not obsessive. Showing sound restraint and confidence is important, as is a healthy dose of respect for the time and privacy of admissions office staff.

Where's the Money?

Where's the Money?

If ever you need the support of a community net-work—both online and off—it's while trying to sort out college finances. Though this is the last chapter in this book, it is certainly not the least important. For some students and their families, it may feel like financial aid should be the first thing they should do toward getting to college. The truth is, you should not limit your school search only to schools that you think you can afford. You should create your short list of colleges before you start to worry about the cost. Only when you know what schools you are shooting for, can you have an idea of your dollar requirements. The tuition for colleges and universities varies greatly, but generally speaking, the schools with higher tuitions offer greater financial aid awards. And there are many,

many sources of scholarships for the student who is willing to do the legwork.

– 24 –
Find Financial Aid Online

The financial aid and scholarship processes involve lots of forms and steps and the gathering of personal information. It can be overwhelming for student and parents alike. The best way to go about the task is to take a deep breath and dive in. The college official Web sites all have a dedicated financial-aid page. For most universities, admissions and financial aid go hand-in-hand, so their financial-aid page tab will feature prominently on their admissions page. This doesn't mean that colleges base their admissions decisions on your financial condition. To the contrary, most schools have a "need-blind" admissions process. But since the financial aid process takes time, most schools encourage applicants to begin to prepare as soon as possible.

So the first step toward pursuing financial aid is to find the financial aid discussion on the college Web site pages of the schools to which you are applying and follow their directions precisely. If you are finding the process bewildering, as many do, seek help. You may discover that connecting with the schools' financial aids offices is difficult, which is not uncommon (those offices are very busy places). But not to worry, there are lots of places to go online for information.

The financial aid effort really requires a twofold attack. You want to stay on top of the school financial aid process, and you want to seek and apply for scholarships and grants from other sources. You, along with your parents, as a team, should decide to go for every dollar and every opportunity for college money. And social media, believe it or not, can help.

Generally, the two kinds of financial aid Web sites coincide with your twofold effort to get the most from your school and from outside sources. There are Web sites and blogs that can help you take the process apart, learn the necessary steps, and connect with others who can exchange information and commiserate with you. Other sites help you find and apply for scholarships. These scholarship search sites use the social network model to gather information about you and use it to find scholarships, grants, and contests that match your circumstances and accomplishments. There are Web sites that attempt to do a little of both, but most sites fall into one of these two categories with regard to their main focus.

General information and how-to sites abound that simplify the financial aid process and provide general information about ways to get money for college. CollegeFinancialAidGuide.com is one such site. It offers an exhaustive list of subject matter to completely cover financial aid and related topics. SallieMaeFund. org is another site that attempts to demystify the financial aid process and provide the tools to successfully find and acquire funds for college. SallieMae-Fund.org is a sort of combination information site and scholarship site. It provides lists of scholarships for specific groups, like African-American and Latino students. But its sister site, smfscholarships.com, is a full-on personalized scholarship search site, like the ones discussed below.

Fastweb.com, FindTuition.com, and BrokeScholar.com are other examples of personalized scholarship search sites. By now, you are very familiar with this social network model. In order to use them, you must join or register on the site. Your personal information is collected on a profile page, and that information is used to connect you with resources and other members with a similar interest. In order to be matched with scholarships amassed in these search site directories, you will again need to take the steps to register and join. And though you may have site registration fatigue by now, the effort is well worth the time because these scholarship matching sites take the mystery and the hours of research out of the scholarship search process. The more detail you can put into your profile, the better your scholarship matches will fit your situation. You want your search to yield as many results as possible to increase your options and opportunities. The site will supply you with a list of scholarships, their requirements, qualifications, deadlines, and reward amounts. Once your list of possible awards is generated, the site will email you reminders of the deadlines for the awards on your list. In addition, most of these search sites will continue to search for scholarships and then alert you by email when they uncover additional awards that match you. Many of the sites offer other services that use your information to assist you. Some have job listings. Some offer college matching functions. Many offer forum discussions so that you can interact with and exchange information with other students who are in the midst of their searches, too. Most of these sites provide articles and expert advice on how to manage your college money.

You can find an exhaustive directory of scholarship search sites at Scholarships.com/free_scholarship_searches.htm. You really only need to join one scholarship search site, since they are all generally drawing from the same pool of awards. If you are in the military, however, you might register at one of the larger sites, like FastWeb.com and also a site that caters only to military personnel, like http://www.mcs-fex.net/Default.aspx. This applies to any other special interest group. If you find a site in the directory that includes scholarships for a specialty or unique situation that applies to you (such as for artists or for study abroad), register there as well as a general search site.

Financial aid blogs can also be helpful. There are bloggers who post about new scholarships or scholarships whose deadlines are approaching, like ScholarshipOffers.net. Some bloggers give advice about how to approach the financial aid process. Often these blogs are created by admissions officers, like FinancialAidBlog.blogspot.com/, which is written by Joe Dobrota, Director of Virginia's Regent University financial aid office. Some blogs are sponsored by university financial aid offices and manned by their staffs, like John Carroll University's Financial Aid Blog at JCUblog.typepad.com/financial_aid_blog/.

These blogs tend to focus on the deadlines and updates for their specific schools. They can be helpful as you are applying to the particular school and entering their financial aid process, but they also offer articles that clarify general financial aid and scholarship questions and commonly encountered problems.

Social networking for financial aid can turn an onerous, complicated, and sometimes mystifying process into a much more transparent and less isolating one. You still have to put in quite a bit of effort to gather and organize your financial information and to meet deadlines, but with Web sites that show you the steps to financial aid and that find and sort through all of the potential awards for you, your time, effort, and stress level are greatly reduced, while your opportunities are substantially enhanced.

Aren't you glad you are a college applicant now instead of in the Dark Ages when your parents were high school students? You have enormously powerful tools in your social media arsenal to use for your college admissions process. Make sure you use them to your benefit—to increase your positive exposure online, connect with your schools of choice, and find money in ways that reduce your effort and increase your chances of success.

Note to Parents

The college application process can be difficult for high school juniors and seniors to handle on their own. In fact, most kids are not prepared to successfully navigate the necessary steps to finding, applying to schools, and deciphering the financial aid process without the help of adults. Though you may feel that you need to take over the entire college application process, you really are in a better position to take on a managerial role, helping your child organize his materials and information and to keep track of deadlines. Colleges want to receive college applications that reflect the student's own opinions and life. Many college admissions officers say that they can recognize an application that has been completed by a parent instead of the student almost immediately. These applications are discarded. If you help your child structure his process by providing a designated space for his materials and helping him keep up with his calendar of due dates, you will free up his time and help him stay clearheaded about his progress. This way, he can really focus on the content of his applications and on putting his best foot forward—on his own.

The financial aid part of the application process, however, requires more involvement on the parent's part. This is where you can focus your own time (and excess nervous energy!). Since your child's financial aid awards will likely be based on your financial information, you will be asked to fill out some of the paperwork and online forms. Also, since you are likely the person who will be responsible for paying for any shortfall in aid, you want to make sure that you and your child have pursued every opportunity for assistance. Nearly all of the financial aid and scholarship Web sites encourage active involvement by parents. You can register as a parent and create your own profile, so that you can actively take part in the search and information gathering functions. This is highly advisable if financial aid is a big factor for your child's college possibilities. Visit the sites. Find out what is expected of you as a parent and make sure all of the necessary information is thorough. Start early to increase your child's chances for greater financial aid awards.

I know an enterprising mother who began to explore financial aid and scholarships for her child when her daughter was in middle school. She began by researching all of the local organizations that sponsored scholarships, beginning with those she already had affiliations with. She involved her child with organizations that offered scholarships to participants. And she began to take her child on visits to colleges so that her daughter could start thinking about the kind of school she wanted to attend. By the time her daughter was ready to graduate from high school, she had amassed more than $100,000 in scholarship money and had so many scholarship awards that they turned some away! This smart mother was able to accomplish all of this without the Internet! Imagine what could be done with the help of all of the social media tools and online resources at your disposal!

Be proactive.

Start early.

Use your tools.

Best of Luck!

Appendix 1:
A Word About Safety

Appendix 1:
A Word About Safety

For much of this book, students are encouraged to share their personal information in multiple locations (and in many forms) all over the Internet. Even though many of the Web sites discussed herein have well-established security and privacy policies, there is no denying that the sharing of information online comes with inherent risks, especially for teenagers and young adults.

What is at risk? When you put your personal information out into the Interweb sphere, you risk encountering the following:

1. Predators
2. Cyber-bullies
3. Phishing and other security theft concerns
4. All manner of dishonesty and deceit

Predators—pedophiles and online stalkers—are the first name in online danger and risk. They are often the first kind of assault that comes to mind when contemplating how to safeguard yourself in your Internet comings and goings. The disturbing reality about online predators is that you often don't discover their deception until it's too late. Just recently a seventeen-year-old British teen was killed by a man she met on Facebook. She thought, based on his false profile, that he was sixteen. But as it turns out, he was a thirty-two-year-old registered sex offender.[1] The victim's mother told reporters that she was confident her daughter did not connect with "friends" she didn't know. She said they had often discussed online safety. And yet, the victim took the chance to meet this new friend instead of going to spend the night with a girl-friend.[2]

Though most Web sites have installed some safety measures to reduce predatory activity, as long as someone can sign on with an alternate identity, which is possible on every social media site, users are in danger of being misled by dangerous people. Teens are most at risk when they friend people they do not know. A young, new acquaintance may not feel like a stranger when his profile has an attractive picture and discloses interests in common with your own. But he is a stranger and he may not be who he says he is. Do not friend strangers and do not arrange meetings with people you do not know separately from your social media connection. They may seem to be the person of your dreams, but the reality of who they really are could be far different.

To reduce your risk, you should take the following steps:

1. Never disclose your contact information—address, phone number, ideally, not even your school.
2. Never disclose your current location or where you plan on going. Avoid social mapping sites, like Foursquare.com, that allow you to publicly post your current location.

3. Never disclose personal information about family, such as where your parents work.
4. Be careful posting pictures that identify your location or places you frequent.
5. Do not respond to emails or text messages requesting personal information from anyone you do not know personally.
6. Become a privacy settings expert. Know what your settings are and use them to control access to your pages.
7. When you join a Facebook group or any other kind of forum, you are interacting with people you do not know. Predators love these kinds of open formats. Leave your group acquaintances in the groups, and do not friend them unless you know them. Be wary of group members who single you out, give you unusual attention, or try to lead you off of the group topic.

Cyberbullying: According to the Cyberbullying Research Center, a Web site founded by two criminologists, cyberbullying occurs "when someone repeatedly harasses, mistreats, or makes fun of another person online or while using cell phones or other electronic devices."[3] Most studies conducted on the prevalence of bullying online consistently show that it is not just common, but rampant. According to the National Crime Prevention Center, 43 percent of teens have experienced cyberbullying in the last year.[4] The most common way teens have been victimized is by an online contact pretending to be someone else in order to trick them into revealing personal information. The next most common offense is when someone spreads untruths about them to others. The more places you share your information, the greater your chances of encountering a bully. In order to reduce your risk, take the following steps:

1. However tempting it may be, do not respond to cyberbullies. Delete messages without reading them. This will help you avoid the temptation to respond and discourage the bully from continuing.

2. Block the bullies' messages. Most social media sites have a way to block specific users from your pages. According to National Crime Prevention Web site, 70 percent of cyberbullying victims said using the block function was the most effective method of prevention.
3. Report incidents to Internet service providers and Web site moderators.
4. Tell a parent or a trusted adult.
5. Be sure to keep your passwords secret from everyone, except your parents.
6. If the incidents involve threats of physical harm or harassment, call the police.
7. Take these actions as soon as possible, to avoid escalation.[5]

Phishing: Scammers are phishing when they send out e-mails that appear to come from legitimate Web sites—such as banks or credit card companies. In the email, you are asked to provide your personal information in order to update or validate your account, or in order to receive something "for free." In this way, the scammer attempts to get hold of your usernames and passwords, address, phone number, your Social Security number, or credit card number. The tricky aspect of these attacks is that they imitate popular or well-established Web sites to gain access information. According to www.Mashable.com, a Web site that keeps its finger on the pulse of the computer world, Facebook is the number-four top site for phishing attacks, following Paypal, eBay, and HSBC. This means that you can get an attack email claiming to be a Facebook promotion or event. And who wants to miss out on a Facebook event?

Phishing is a form of identity theft. Thirty-one percent of reported identity theft victims are young people, because teens have good credit ratings and very little debt. In order to avoid phishers and other scammers, take the following precautions:

1. Never share personal information. Perhaps this warning has been repeated some 20 times in

this book so far, because it is that important. Do not share your address, phone number, hometown, or school anywhere online unless you have checked the Web site's security.

2. Don't trust email solicitations. Never give sensitive information in response to an email or after following a link in an email.

3. Log off of public computers. This includes the library, your school, or any cyber-cafe computer.

4. Create secure passwords and keep them secret. Some sites give your password a security rating as you are registering. If the site says your password is a poor choice, change it until you get a stronger rating.

5. Learn to recognize and report fraud. Look out for the warning signs of identity fraud, such as emails or solicitations from preapproved credit card companies or banks, collection agencies, or suspicious companies that imitate legitimate ones. If you suspect that your identity has been

compromised, tell your parents immediately and take action to limit the damage. Contact all credit card companies, banks, all three credit reporting agencies (TransUnion, Equifax, and Experian), and the police. Change your passwords for all online accounts. Keep records of all the remedial actions that you have taken.

Dishonesty and Deceit: All of these Internet security dangers boil down to dishonesty and deceit. The most important thing you can remember—the Internet rule that takes precedence over all others—is do not believe everything you read, see, or hear online: that cute girl who wants to friend you, that too-good-to-be-true email deal offer, that gossip on your Facebook wall about a mutual acquaintance. When it comes to information from people and places you do not know personally, look it over carefully with extra scrutiny. And communicate any suspicious behavior to your parents.

Facebook privacy settings and college admissions

visitors: Chapters 19 and 21 discuss the Facebook privacy settings in detail, but if you want to lock down your social media page more securely, you should not be concerned about shutting out the colleges that you want to attract. You want your colleges of choice to find you, but on your own terms. Restrict your Facebook to "Friends Only" across the board and then you can direct the colleges of interest to your site yourself. There is no guarantee that they will not gain access to your page in other ways—like through mutual friends—but at least you have not put yourself at greater risk in an attempt to increase your exposure for colleges.

As a college applicant, you are taking a step into adulthood. You can take your time to make this transition in many areas of your life, but not in social media. When it comes to social media, the transition needs to happen as soon as you decide you are going to apply to college, for a scholarship, or for a job. I asked Susan Getgood what she thought was the most important thing young adults should know about maintaining their privacy while actively promoting their strengths and accomplishments on social media. Susan Getgood is Managing Director and co-founder of Blog With Integrity and founder of GetGood Strategic Marketing. She has, since the early 1990s, watched the Web evolve from the first browsers to the interactive communities we participate in today. She is an expert in Internet marketing, and businesspeople of all walks of life come to her to find out how to put their best face forward online. Susan has this to say to young adults about social media, safety, and decision making:

> Once you hit seventeen or eighteen, you have to think about Facebook as a place where your personal and professional lives will meet. Your social media is no longer just about fooling around with your friends—no longer a private playground. . . . So go through your Facebook profile and really think about how you want to use this tool. Really look at your privacy settings

and adjust them to fit how you use Facebook and how you want to be seen. Optimally, you will only show personal things to people you know.

As a young adult, using Facebook and other social media responsibly and maturely requires adopting the kind of careful content management discussed throughout this book. The steps you have taken in furtherance of your college admissions will serve you well into your future because people who can significantly influence your goals and your future are online and they are watching.

Be smart and be safe!

Appendix 2:
24 Social Media Abbreviations You Should Know

Appendix 2:
24 Social Media
Abbreviations You Should Know

Thanks to Instant Messaging, these abbreviations have become commonplace among social media users. There is nothing wrong with using abbreviations to express yourself in most cases. If you are composing a post for your blog and your goal is to showcase your writing skills, you should probably communicate in long form and not in this abbreviated style. But in casual conversation—in personal status updates and comments on your social media, you should feel free to use them. Be creative and humorous and be yourself.

Just as you are avoiding all forms of profanity, avoid abbreviations that stand for profane words. Here

are 24 that don't include a single word of profanity!
You can view more at http://www.imacronyms.com.

1. AFAIK: As far as I know
2. AFK: Away from keyboard
3. BBL: Be back Later
4. LOL: Laugh out loud
5. TTYL: Talk to you later
6. G2G: Got to go
7. OMG: Oh my Gosh!
8. SMH: Shaking my head
9. RME: Rolling my eyes
10. ROFL: Rolling on the floor laughing
11. BRB: Be right back
12. BFF: Best friends forever
13. IBTD: I beg to differ
14. IDK: I don't know
15. JIC: Just in case
16. JK: Just kidding
17. BTW: By the way
18. BTB: By the by

19. NVM: never mind
20. NM: Nothing much
21. NBD: No big deal
22. OIC: Oh, I see
23. OBV: obviously
24. THX: thanks

Appendix 3:
24 Places to Go Online

Appendix 3:
24 Places to Go Online

College Review Sites

1. CampusBuddy.com
2. Cappex.com
3. CollegeConfidential.com
4. CollegeProwler.com
5. Ecampustours.com
6. StuVu.com
7. Unigo.com

College Admissions Help Sites

8. MyCollegeGuide.org
9. CollegeAdmissionsWeb.com
10. NotJustAdmissions.com

11. CollegeOfYourDreams.com
12. RethinkingAdmissions.blogs.wfu.edu

Financial Aid and Scholarship Sites

13. Scholarships.com
14. FinAid.org/scholarships
15. IEFA.org
16. College-Scholarships.com/free_scholarship_searches.htm
17. Brokescholar.com
18. FindTuition.com
19. HowToGetIn.com

Safety Sites

20. AThinLine.org
21. ConnectSafely.org
22. WiredSafety.org
23. NetSmartz.org/netteens.htm
24. Microsoft.com/protect/

Notes

Notes

Introduction

1. Marc Zucherberg, "Six Years of Making Facebook." Facebook. Facebook, Web. http://blog.facebook.com/blog.php?post=287542162130, February 4, 2010.

2. Susannah Fox and Amanda Lenhart, "Bloggers: A Portrait of the Internet's New Storytellers," Pew Internet & American Life Project, Pew Research Center, http://www.pewinternet.org/~/media/Files/Reports/2006/PIP%20Bloggers%20Report%20July%2019%202006.pdf.pdf, July 19, 2006.

A Simple Plan

1. Nora Ganim-Barnes and Eric Mattson, Social Media and College Admissions: The First Longitu-

dinal Study, University of Massachusetts Dartmouth Center for Marketing Research, http://www.umassd.edu/cmr/studiesresearch/mediaandadmissions.cfm, 2009.

**The College Search—
Finding Your Soul-Mate School**

1. See The Best College Rankings Web site for a discussion of the *U.S. News & World Report* list and others, http://bestcollegerankings.org/popular-rankings/us-news-world-report-college-rankings/
2. *Princeton Review*'s List of the top 371 colleges in the country, http://www.princetonreview.com/rankingsbest.aspx

Chapter 1
1. Abby McCartney, "When Choosing A College, What Really Matters?" Unigo/WSJ On Campus,

http://www.unigo.com/articles/when_choosing_a_college,_what_really_matters%5E63/?taxonomyId=760028, September 18, 2009.

Chapter 2
1. http://www.uh.edu/about/houston.
2. http://www.virtualtourist.com/travel/North_America/United_States_of_America/Texas/Houston-878298/Warnings_or_Dangers-Houston-Weather_Wise-BR-1.html#5.

Chapter 4
1. http://www.unigo.com/elon_university/reviews/24491/
2. Collegeprowler.com's Personality Quiz, https://collegeprowler.com/account/editpersonality.aspx

Chapter 5
1. "Social Networking Sites and College-Bound Students," StudentPoll, College Board and Art &

Science Group, LLC., http://professionals.colleg-eboard.com/data-reports-research/trends/studentpoll/social-networking, 2009.

Chapter 7
1. American Marketing Association's online dictionary, http://www.marketingpower.com/_layouts/Dictionary.aspx

Chapter 8
1. Tim Wilkinson and Marianne Lill, "Judging a Book by Its Cover: Descriptive Survey of Patients' Preferences for Doctors' Appearance and Mode of Address," http://www.bmj.com/cgi/content/abstract/331/7531/1524 (2005); Jorn P. W. Scharlemann, Catherine C. Eckel, Alex Kacelnik, Rick K. Wilson, "The Value of a Smile: Game Theory with a Human Face," *Journal of Economic Psychology* 22, issue 5 (2001): 617-40.
2. Murray Feingold, "Dr. Murray Feingold: Judging People by Their Physical Appearance," Wicked Local Dedham, Gatehouse News Service,

http://www.dailynewstranscript.com/entertainment/
x201790920/Dr-Murray-Feingold-Judging-people-
by-their-physical-appearance, January 19, 2010.

Chapter 17
1. Andrew Flagel, "Yes or No to Video with Your
College Application," The Fat Envelope blog, My-
CollegeOptions.org, http://www.mycollegeoptions.
org/BlogEngine/post/2010/04/video-college-applica-
tion.aspx, April 14, 2010.

2. Tamar Lewin, "To Impress, Tufts Prospects
Turn To YouTube," *New York Times,* http://www.
nytimes.com/2010/02/23/education/23tufts.html,
February 10, 2010.

The Online Makeover
1. "Can What You Post on Facebook Prevent
You from Getting into College?" Video webcast, Unigo.com and WSJCampus.com, http://
www.unigo.com/articles/can_what_you_post_

on_facebook_prevent_you_from_getting_into_
college^63/?taxonomyId=760030, December 7,
2009.

Chapter 19

1. The Retrevo Gadgetology Report, "Preserve
Your Facebook Privacy, Post Cautiously," Retrevo
Blog http://www.retrevo.com/content/blog/2010/05/
preserve-your-facebook-privacy-post-cautiously,
May 13, 2010.

Chapter 20

1. "Can What You Post on Facebook Prevent
You from Getting into College?" Video webcast, Unigo.com and WSJCampus.com, http://
www.unigo.com/articles/can_what_you_post_
on_facebook_prevent_you_from_getting_into_
college^63/?taxonomyId=760030, December 7,
2009.

Chapter 23

1. Kaplan Annual Survey of College Admissions Officials, cited by Lindsey Anderson, "To Friend or Not to Friend? College Admissions in the Age of Facebook," *USA Today,* http://www.usatoday.com/news/education/2009-09-16-facebook-admissions_N.htm, September 18, 2009.

A Word About Safety

1. Jeremy Armstrong, "I killed a girl": What drifter suspected of murdering teenager Ashleigh Hall told police, the *Mirror,* Mirror.co.uk http://www.mirror.co.uk/most-popular/2009/10/28/i-killed-a-girl-what-drifter-suspected-of-murdering-teenager-ashleigh-hall-told-police-115875-21778255/, 10/28/2009.

2. James Tozer, "Mother of teenage girl killed 'after meeting man on Facebook' calls for ban on false online profiles," Mail Online, the Associated Newspapers, http://bx.businessweek.com/mobile-social-networking/mother-of-teenage-girl-

killed-after-meeting-man-on-facebook-calls-for-ban-on-false-online-profiles/2442597363472425888-7a445d68111b01e667ff56623292ea8f/, 10/31/2009.

3. Justin W. Patchin, "Defining Cyberbullying," The Cyberbullying Research Center Blog, http://cyberbullying.us/blog/tag/defining-cyberbullying, September 22, 2008.

4. Stop Cyberbullying Before It Starts, National Crime Prevention Council, http://www.ncpc.org/resources/files/pdf/bullying/cyberbullying.pdf.

5. Ibid.

Check out these other books in the **good things to know** series:

5 Things to Know for Successful and Lasting Weight Loss
(ISBN: 9781596525580, $9.99)

12 Things to Do to Quit Smoking
(ISBN: 9781596525849, $9.99)

Sorry For Your Loss: What People Who Are Grieving Wish You Knew
(ISBN: 9781596527478, $9.99)

20 Things To Know About Divorce
(ISBN: 9781596525993, $9.99)

21 Things To Create a Better Life
(ISBN: 9781596525269, $9.99)

27 Things To Feng Shui Your Home
(ISBN: 9781596525672, $9.99)

27 Things To Know About Yoga
(ISBN: 9781596525900, $9.99)

29 Things To Know About Catholicism
(ISBN: 9781596525887, $9.99)

30 Things Future Dads Should Know About Pregnancy
(ISBN: 9781596525924, $9.99)

33 Things To Know About Raising Creative Kids
(ISBN: 9781596525627, $9.99)

34 Things To Know About Wine
(ISBN: 9781596525894, $9.99)

35 Things to Know to Raise Active Kids
(ISBN: 9781596525870, $9.99)

35 Things Your Teen Won't Tell You, So I Will
(ISBN: 9781596525542, $9.99)

37 Things To Know About Grammar
(ISBN: 9781596525863, $9.99)

41 Things To Know About Autism
(ISBN: 9781596525832, $9.99)

44 Things Parents Should Know About Healthy Cooking For Kids
(ISBN: 9781596527447, $9.99)

46 Things You Can Do To Help Your Teen Manage Stress
(ISBN: 9781596527416, $9.99)

48 Things To Know About Sustainable Living
(ISBN: 9781596527409, $9.99)

51 Things You Should Know Before Getting Engaged
(ISBN: 9781596525481, $9.99)

52 Things Brides on a Budget Should Know
(ISBN: 9781596525931, $9.99)

52 Things To Pick Up Your Poker Game
(ISBN: 9781596525917, $9.99)

70 Things First-time Homebuyers Need To Know
(ISBN: 9781596526006, $9.99)

99 Things to Save Money in Your Household Budget
(ISBN: 9781596525474, $9.99)

Contact Turner Publishing at (615) 255-2665
or visit turnerpublishing.com
to get your copies today!

Printed in the USA
CPSIA information can be obtained
at www.ICGtesting.com
JSHW052015140824
68134JS00027B/2488